P9-CIS-441

362.7
Nag   Nagi
               Child maltreatment in
           the United States

**GLENDALE COLLEGE
LIBRARY**

DEMCO

DISCARD

 Child Maltreatment in the United States

CHILD MALTREATMENT IN THE UNITED STATES

A Challenge to Social Institutions

SAAD Z. NAGI

New York COLUMBIA UNIVERSITY PRESS *1977*

Library of Congress Cataloging in Publication Data
Nagi, Saad Zaghloul.
  Child maltreatment in the United States.

  Includes bibliographical references and index.
  1. Child abuse—United States.   2. Child abuse—
United States—Prevention.   3. Child welfare—United
States.   I. Title.
HV741.N23   362.7'1   77-22121
ISBN 0-231-04394-5

362.7
Nag

Copyright © 1977 Columbia University Press
All rights reserved.
Columbia University Press
New York   Guildford, Surrey
Printed in the United States of America

6/79

To
Kay and Karima,
Mazen, and Omar

PREFACE

THE BACKGROUND of this work may help to replace it in perspective. It represents an important part of broader research interests pursued for a number of years at the Mershon Center, Ohio State University, in the structure and performance of agencies administering human services. Interest on the part of sponsors of the study was generated in response to legislation then pending that has become the Child Abuse Prevention and Treatment Act of 1974. The information available when the legislation was initiated was not sufficient to serve as a basis for inferences concerning the problem of child maltreatment and its handling nationwide. This work, therefore, was designed to mobilize concepts and data in ways that would go beyond description and explanation to provide some basis for policy and program development. The path to such development is still largely uncharted and is fraught with difficulties.

It is with great appreciation that I acknowledge the sponsorship of this work by the Children's Bureau of the Office of Child Development (now the Administration on Children, Youth, and Families) of the U.S. Department of Health, Education, and Welfare. The openness, cooperation, and substantive contributions of members of these agencies made a difficult task rewarding and pleasant. Vital to my inquiry was the University of Michigan's Survey Research Center, which undertook the sampling and the collection and preparation of data. Also of vital importance were the many respondents who shared with me their time and thought.

Many individuals made substantive and other contributions to the inquiry and to this study. Acknowledgments are due Douglas Besharov, Frank Ferro, Charles Gershenson, Helen Howerton, and Cecilia Sudia, of the Children's Bureau and the Office of Child Development of the U.S. Department of Health, Education, and Welfare, Frederick Green and Sally Ryan, formerly of the Children's Bureau; and Irene Hess, Jeanne Keresztesi, Joan Scheffler, John Scott, and John Siebs, of the University of Michigan's Survey Research Center.

I am indebted to the intellectual stimulation of colleagues Ronald Corwin, Harold Lasswell, William Petersen, and Richard Snyder. My gratitude is also extended to members of the research group that worked on the study: Richard Haller and his colleagues Bruce Jonas, Ted Smith, and Eve Pease, who handled data computation and analysis competently and diligently; Lisa Ede, who made the manuscript readable; John Diamond, Semra Somersan, and John Myers, who assisted in the research; and Evelyn Rist and Nedra Story, who responded to the pressures of manuscript preparation with high standards and good humor.

Columbus, Ohio
May, 1976

CONTENTS

Child Maltreatment in the United States

ABBREVIATIONS

CPS	Child Protective Services
CRT	Juvenile and Family Courts
GAO	General Accounting Office
HMD	Hospital Medical Personnel
HSS	Hospital Social Services Departments
SCAN	Screening Child Abuse and Neglect
SCH	School Systems
PHN	Public Health Nursing Agencies
POL	Police and Sheriff's Departments
WATS	Wide Area Telecommunication Service

CHAPTER ONE

BACKGROUND AND SCOPE, PROBLEM AND APPROACHES

WITH CHILD MALTREATMENT as with most social problems, the growth of public awareness and concern preceded both the development of legal codes and the intervention of the state through active services and law enforcement programs.[1] The nineteenth century witnessed many reform movements spearheaded by religious organizations and by other voluntary groups. During the first half of that century, houses for poor and neglected children were opened in New York, some with private support and others with a mix of private and public funding. During the second half of the century, societies for the prevention of cruelty to animals began also to take note of abused and neglected children. New organizations and new sections in established organizations were developed specifically for the prevention of cruelty to children. Medical recognition of child abuse was introduced in 1888 "in a paper on acute periosteal swelling in infants."[2] In 1889 a juvenile court was established in Chicago, although "the legal presumption of the courts," at that time, "was generally in favor of the reasonableness of parental action."[3] New professions concerned with children and families, such as child psychology and social work, also emerged around the turn of the century.

Efforts on behalf of maltreated children, as well as concern over child welfare in general, culminated in the First White House Conference on Children, held in 1909. The conference was followed in 1912 by legislation initiating the Children's Bureau, a public agency established to investigate and report upon "all matters pertaining to the welfare of children and child life among all classes of people."[4] Title IVB ("Child Welfare Services") of the 1935 Social Security Act represented further development of public programs in this area,[5] although its child protection aspects remained underdeveloped and diffused into other social services.

The 1960s and the early 1970s were marked by both heightened public awareness and by the mobilization òf interests to protect children against abuse and neglect. During this period, a voluminous literature concerning this problem accumulated in medicine, law, social services, and the behavioral sciences.[6] The mass media played an important role in sensitizing the public at large. In 1962, amendments to the Social Security Act "required each state to develop a plan to extend child welfare services, including protective services, to every political subdivision."[7] The same year saw the issuance of a model law—that is, a suggested form for legislation—on the reporting of abuse and neglect; its language was adopted by most of the states within the following two years.[8] During the latter part of the decade, many states either introduced new laws or reformed existing ones to require reporting by certain professions and to lift legal liability for unsubstantiated reports.[9]

The most dramatic results were achieved by Florida, which not only changed the statutes, but also installed toll-free 24-hour WATS lines and mounted an effective campaign of public information through the mass media. Within a period of one year, the number of reported cases increased from 17 to 19,120.[10] From 1971 to 1974 these stabilized at between 25,000 and 30,000 annually; approximately 60 percent of these reports were substantiated upon investigation by responsible agencies.[11] Most states made similar legislative changes, and a number of communities in the United States increased their efforts toward case identification.

During the early 1970s, the problem of child abuse and neglect entered the political agenda on the national level. In 1973, the Department of Health, Education, and Welfare assigned the Office of Child Development the task of coordinating the efforts of the National Institute of Mental Health, the Public Health Services, the Office of Education, and the Rehabilitation Services Administration in regard to this problem.[12] In 1974 the Child Abuse Prevention and Treatment law was enacted. One of its provisions established the National Center on Child Abuse and Neglect; it also funded a number of demonstration programs and projects in various parts of the country "designed to prevent, identify, and treat child abuse and neglect."[13] Amendments to the Social Security Act in 1975 introduced Title XX, which also provided for grants to the states for services to children and families. In addition to its other purposes, this title was addressed to "preventing or remedying neglect, abuse, or exploitation of children and adults unable to protect their own interests, or preserving, rehabilitating, or reuniting families."[14]

It was within the context of these legislative activities and administrative concerns, as well as heightened public and professional awareness, that work on this volume was initiated in January, 1974.

Deliberation over policies and programs indicated that, with few exceptions, information was sorely lacking on important aspects of child maltreatment. The exceptions included a comprehensive survey, published in 1974, of the status of legislation concerning the problem in the various states,[15] as well as several publications in pediatrics, radiology, and in related medical and health fields on technical developments in the diagnosis and treatment of victims of abuse and neglect.[16] But current estimates of the severity of the problem were viewed skeptically, since reported cases of socially unacceptable and legally liable behavior are usually assumed to represent only the tip of the iceberg. In fact, because neither therapeutic nor law-enforcement agencies had actively sought out cases, it was suspected that the submerged portions of the iceberg for this problem might be even larger than for other forms of deviant behavior. Given these limitations in case identification, the state of epidemiological knowledge remained anecdotal and primitive. Some case studies of given communities or programs were reported and others were under way; most, however, lacked a comparative perspective and the requisites for generalizability.

This study was planned to address some of the gaps in available information. Its purposes were: to gain an analytical, nationally representative picture of the organization of services and control mechanisms concerned with child abuse and neglect; to identify limitations and strengths in the structure and performance of these programs; and to prepare recommendations for improving the identification and control of the problem. The presentation of findings is organized around these objectives, and is preceded by a discussion of important contextual issues, dilemmas in the field, and estimates of the magnitude and dimensions of the problem. Before turning to these parts of the report, however, we will review the methodological steps followed.

METHODOLOGICAL APPROACHES

The study was planned around three interlocking segments. The first consisted of intensive interviews in a number of communities selected on the basis of variability. These interviews were conducted with judges, physicians, members of police departments, caseworkers, public health nurses, and others in organizations encountering child abuse and neglect. We also attended court proceedings and toured pediatric wards and other facilities. The objective in this phase was to gain an understanding of the issues, problems, weaknesses, and strengths that characterize programs in the field—necessary background information both in the development of a meaningful conceptual framework for a national survey and in the interpretation of its results. In addition, this information constituted an important source of suggestions for program development.

The second segment of this work involved a survey of organizations and programs related to abuse and neglect. The selection of organizations and respondents surveyed was based upon a probability sample of the United States population. Seven agencies and groups of respondents serving this sample were included in the survey. Data were collected through personal interviews. These organizations and respondents comprise the social, legal, educational, and health institutions most often involved with families and children when maltreatment occurs. The following is an account of these organizations

and of our criteria and priorities for the selection of respondents
within each.

Child Protective Services (CPS): Interviewed were directors or
supervisors of these agencies or divisions, and the most knowledgeable members of the staff if the director or supervisor had
not completed six months or more in the agency.

Juvenile and Family Courts (CRT): Interviewed were judges or
court referees, when judges felt the latter were more appropriate
sources of information.

Police and Sheriff's Departments (POL): Interviewed were heads
of juvenile divisions, if existent, and the heads of departments if
no such divisions existed.

Public Health Nursing Agencies (PHN): Interviewed were supervisors of maternal and child nursing services, if such a specialization existed and, if not, the directors of nursing services in
general.

School Systems (SCH): Interviewed were assistant superin-
tendents for pupil personnel or persons in equivalent positions.

Hospital Medical Personnel (HMD): Respondents in this group
were selected according to the following priorities: pediatricians
who headed or participated in hospital teams or special programs; if no such program existed, heads of pediatric departments; if no pediatric department existed, pediatricians most
knowledgeable about child abuse and neglect; and if no pediatri-
cian was available, chiefs of staff in hospitals.

Hospital Social Service Departments (HHS): Interviewed were
heads of these departments or their most knowledgeable
members if heads had not been in hospitals for six months or
more.

Throughout the survey emphasis was placed upon reaching persons informed about their respective programs. Respondents were to
act as informants on what they perceived the programs to be, rather
than what they believed they should be. A total of 1,696 interviews
was completed, representing 96.4 percent of the respondents sought.
As shown in Table 1.1, the highest completion rates were for police

TABLE 1.1
ORGANIZATIONS COMPLETING INTERVIEWS, WITH COMPLETION RATES

Types of Organizations	Number of Organizations	Interviews Completed	Rates of Completion
Child protective services	130	129	99.2
Public health nursing agencies	151	148	98.0
School systems	339	330	97.3
Hospital medical personnel	388	350	90.2
Hospital social services	325	317	97.5
Juvenile and family courts	137	134	97.8
Police and sheriff's departments	290	288	99.3
Totals	1,760	1,696	96.4

and sheriff's departments (99.3 percent), child protective services (99.2 percent), and public health nursing agencies (98 percent), with the lowest for hospital medical personnel (90.2 percent).

The sampling design and the selection of organizations were based upon a probability sample of 8,090 household units located within 1,680 sampling segments selected for an earlier survey conducted by this investigator.[17] These segments were used as points of departure for sampling the organizations. Each segment falls within the jurisdiction of a child protective agency, a juvenile or a family court, a police or a sheriff's department, a school system, or a public health department. Agencies representing these jurisdictions were selected for interviews. Included also were all children's hospitals within the counties or the Standard Metropolitan Statistical Areas where any of the sampling segments were located. Other hospitals were selected on the basis of accessibility to the household units in the sample, the closest hospitals being considered most accessible. Hospital selection was further limited to those operating emergency rooms and/or accepting pediatric patients.

Responses from the organizations surveyed were weighted according to the number of households that fell within their respective jurisdictions. Thus, reports about a child protective agency selected on the basis of serving 100 households in the population sample were given five times the weight of another serving only 20 household units. Similar weighting was applied to responses from all other agencies. Children's hospitals, which do not fall naturally in the sample selection, were excluded from the weighted results by assigning them a weight of zero. In this sense, the findings represent programs responsible for, or most accessible to, a probability sample of the United States population excluding Alaska and Hawaii. Throughout this report, unless otherwise specified, the percentages shown in the narrative or in tabular forms are of the United States population as projected from the weighted responses in the sample. It is also important to note that, as in all surveys, data for some questions are missing. These came in the form of "non-response" and "non-answer." The latter category designates responses inappropriate for the questions posed. Both categories of missing data were slight in this survey and therefore were presented neither in the tables nor in the distributions cited in the text. Tables are marked, however, when missing data exceeded 5 percent for any of the variables included. It should also be noted that percentages may not always total exactly 100, because figures were rounded off to the first decimal digit. And, in certain tables like those indicating multiple responses by individual respondents, totals need not come to 100.0 or any approximation of that figure.

The third segment of this work concerned the formulation of recommendations for policy and program planning. In the absence of adequately developed design theories to guide this kind of effort in a systematic manner, reliance was placed upon principles of organization, upon information about the weaknesses and strengths of existing programs, and upon the opinions of knowledgeable people. Also, much was learned by analogy from studies concerning other kinds of human services.

ATTRIBUTES OF RESPONDENTS

Some details about the various organizations' respondents might help clarify their sociodemographic composition. A significant proportion of respondents on behalf of public health nursing services (13.3 percent) were physicians. This was more often the case in large communities than in smaller ones. Conversely, 18.8 percent of the respondents from hospital medical departments were nurses in service or administrative positions. Among respondents from the courts: 71.3

percent were judges; 15.5 percent were referees; and the remaining 13.2 percent were probation officers, intake officers, court social workers, or persons occupying other positions in the courts.

Table 1.2 presents the weighted distribution of respondents along a selected number of characteristics. These distributions indicate that only 4.9 percent of all respondents were under 25 years of age, with an additional 17.9 percent between 25 and 34. About one-half of them were 45 or older. Larger proportions of respondents from child protective agencies and hospital social services were in the younger age categories. Conversely, more of the respondents on behalf of courts and school systems were older. Age distributions among respondents from public health nursing agencies were very similar to those from school systems.

Sex distributions conformed to general expectations. Most of the male respondents on behalf of public health nursing services were physicians or public health officials other than nurses. Nurses responding for hospital medical departments, however, inflated the proportion of women in this category. It is interesting to note that women represented the police departments more often in the larger communities. The great majority of all respondents were white, varying from 90.4 percent in public health nursing to 96.7 percent in police and sheriff's departments. Blacks ranged from a low of 1.6 percent for respondents from hospital medical departments to a high of 8.2 percent for public health nursing. Chicanos, American Indians, and Orientals comprised very small proportions of the respondents.

Table 1.2 also indicates that most respondents were married at the time of the survey. The single were more highly represented among members of hospital social services, child protective agencies, and public health nursing services, respectively. The majority of respondents had children, in most cases under 18 years of age. Nevertheless, it should be noted that substantial proportions of the respondents were childless, especially among those participating on behalf of hospital social services, child protective agencies, and public health nursing services. In large part, this is attributable to the greater prevalence of single persons among these respondents.

Educational levels below the bachelor's degree, represented by 16.8 percent of the weighted responses, were generally concentrated

TABLE 1.2
ATTRIBUTES OF RESPONDENTS
(PERCENTAGES)

Attributes of Respondents	Organizations and Respondents						
	CPS	PHN	SCH	HMD	HSS	CRT	POL
Age							
Under 25	5.5	5.0	0.5	2.6	15.0	0.4	7.9
25–34	28.2	12.1	10.5	19.5	34.1	8.4	16.9
35–44	33.4	26.6	32.0	35.3	20.1	20.3	31.5
45–54	24.1	39.9	40.7	27.5	19.4	42.9	32.8
55+	8.8	16.4	16.3	15.0	11.5	28.1	10.8
Sex							
Male	49.7	9.1	64.7	69.5	16.6	89.2	81.6
Female	55.3	90.9	35.3	30.5	83.4	10.8	18.4
Ethnicity							
White	91.7	90.4	91.1	94.3	92.9	94.1	96.7
Black	7.8	8.2	6.8	1.6	5.3	5.9	2.5
Other	0.4	1.4	2.0	4.1	1.7	0.0	0.8
Marital status							
Married	69.8	66.3	85.9	83.2	60.5	90.6	84.8
Separated and divorced	6.0	5.0	4.1	6.3	8.9	4.1	6.1
Widowed	0.0	5.9	2.2	2.5	4.1	1.2	1.1
Single	24.2	22.8	7.7	8.0	26.1	4.1	8.0
Other	0.0	0.0	0.0	0.0	0.4	0.0	0.0
Children							
None	36.6	35.6	18.7	16.4	46.5	6.6	15.6
Under 18 Only	34.4	27.1	29.9	45.6	32.3	30.3	40.5
Over 18 Only	18.7	27.3	27.9	21.0	11.0	39.4	22.0
Both under and over 18	10.3	10.1	23.5	17.0	10.2	23.6	21.9
Education							
Below college	1.1	0.0	1.6	0.0	5.4	3.7	32.1
Some college	4.2	0.0	6.1	0.0	7.7	3.1	48.9
College degree	37.3	1.9	8.2	0.0	35.1	7.1	11.1
Graduate and professional degrees	57.4	98.1	84.0	100.0	51.8	86.1	7.9
Tenure in organization (years)							
1 or less	12.4	9.8	1.2	5.1	17.5	9.8	4.4
2	7.1	7.6	7.7	5.0	22.9	6.4	4.8
3–5	31.4	17.2	14.6	27.7	35.9	24.3	14.7
5–10	18.8	22.1	24.7	19.6	13.9	25.0	21.0
10+	30.2	43.3	51.8	42.6	9.8	34.5	55.0

NOTE: Because percentage figures were rounded off to the first decimal digit, totals in this and subsequent tables may not equal 100.

among respondents from the police. Holders of the bachelor's and master's degrees accounted for 41.3 percent, and were more often to be found in protective agencies and hospital social services. Finally, 41.9 percent of the weighted responses were by persons who had pursued graduate work beyond the master's; this included those who had completed a doctorate or received a professional degree in fields such as medicine or law. As would be expected, the majority of these respondents were from hospital medical departments and from the courts. Most respondents had been in their respective organizations for three years or longer, although not necessarily in the same positions. In fact, excluding respondents from hospital social services, large proportions reported tenures of ten or more years.

TABLE 1.3
THE INTERVIEW SITUATION, WITH INTEREST AND COOPERATION LEVELS
(PERCENTAGES)

Interviewers' Reports	Respondents' Organizations						
	CPS	PHN	SCH	HMD	HSS	CRT	POL
Others Present							
No one	76.7	80.0	79.6	87.3	79.2	87.1	71.6
Respondent's supervisors	6.1	2.2	1.6	1.5	4.8	2.7	2.7
Respondent's colleagues	2.8	5.5	9.0	3.8	5.9	0.4	4.8
Respondent's subordinates	12.1	8.5	7.3	6.9	10.0	7.3	19.3
Others	2.4	3.7	2.5	0.4	0.2	2.4	1.7
Interruptions							
None or Few	54.0	74.7	72.8	64.5	62.8	70.7	50.8
Occasional	35.6	19.9	21.2	26.9	24.2	17.7	35.3
Frequent	10.3	5.4	5.9	8.5	13.0	11.6	13.9
Interest							
Very much interested	75.8	66.5	62.7	48.7	68.3	52.5	62.8
Moderately interested	16.6	28.6	25.9	36.6	21.2	27.8	25.1
Slightly interested	6.3	3.7	8.9	10.2	8.6	14.6	7.0
Not at all interested	1.3	1.2	1.9	3.3	1.6	5.0	4.8
Bored to tears	0.0	0.0	0.7	1.2	0.3	0.1	0.3
Cooperation							
Enthusiastic, positive	76.1	68.2	59.9	47.3	69.6	52.8	66.9
Fairly cooperative	21.6	26.7	31.3	42.2	24.2	33.0	24.3
Neutral	2.3	3.9	7.6	6.4	4.0	8.1	6.4
Somewhat uncooperative	0.0	0.0	0.7	3.6	2.0	4.6	2.0
Hostile or suspicious	0.0	1.2	0.6	0.5	0.1	1.5	0.5

THE INTERVIEW SITUATION

Information concerning interview situations and interviewers' impressions of respondents is seldom presented in reports such as this. Still, comparisons along these lines are instructive. Thus, as we proceed with the presentation of findings, these data will be related to some of the important patterns of responses. Table 1.3 includes information on the interview situation and the levels of interest and cooperation of respondents, as reported by interviewers. The great majority of the interviews were conducted in private; when others were present, they were most often subordinates or colleagues of the respondents. A small proportion of the interviews, ranging from a high of 13.9 percent for the police to a low of 5.4 percent for public health personnel, were frequently interrupted. Most respondents were "moderately" or "very much" interested in the interviews, lack of interest being most common among those from the courts and from hospital medical departments. As would be expected, cooperation was closely associated with interest.

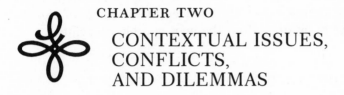

CHAPTER TWO

CONTEXTUAL ISSUES, CONFLICTS, AND DILEMMAS

AN UNDERSTANDING of the structural features and the practical limitations of programs in this field can only be reached within the context of a number of important social dilemmas, value conflicts, and other issues—not all of which are peculiar to problems of child abuse and neglect. This section of the report will identify some of these dilemmas, conflicts, and issues and present related evidence from the survey. To be reviewed are the rights of children and parents and the role of the state, the status of knowledge and technology in the field, incompatibilities between punitive and therapeutic approaches, conflicts within professional roles, and problems arising from the protection of organizational and professional domains.

The positions and opinions of the respondents on the above subjects were sought by eliciting their reactions to a number of statements (Table 2.1). Using a principal component analysis, these statements were further reduced to seven indices by combining those addressing the same issues. The indices and their distributions across organizations and respondents are presented in Table 2.2, which will be referred to at various points throughout this chapter. Before turning to substantive discussions, we need to note two technical observations in regard to these indices: when an index represented only one item, it was presented in a dichotomous fashion by combining the responses "tend to agree" with "strongly agree," and "tend to disagree" with "strongly disagree;" when an index comprised two or more items, it was possible to divide the combined responses into three categories. In dividing the range of the latter types of indices, attempts were made to identify the "natural" clustering of responses rather than draw the lines at arbitrary points.[1]

RIGHTS OF CHILDREN AND PARENTS

Evidence concerning a "natural" or biologically based parent-child tie is at best inconsistent. Lower forms of life manifest conflicting patterns: fish feed on their young, but mothers in other animal species will endanger their own lives to protect their offspring. Human parents' treatment of their children is equally inconsistent; it extends from infanticide on the one extreme to overindulgence on the other. These patterns would hardly constitute convincing evidence that parent-child relations are governed by instincts or intuitions that automatically direct parents to act in the best interests of their children. Nor does our present knowledge of child rearing warrant the assumption that parents always know the best interests of children. But most observers, whatever their conceptions of parent-child relations, would agree that the basic elements in those relations are socially acquired and culturally conditioned. They are altered and modified as the institution of the family changes in response to societal forces.

Historically, responsibility for children, and for other dependents as well, resided largely in primary groups and particularly in the family. The traditional roles of the family, one of the earliest social inventions, have always included both the procreation of children and their care, protection, socialization, and control. The absolute authority of families over their children was vividly expressed by Thomas Hobbes around the middle of the seventeenth century, in the statement that, "like the imbecile, the crazed and the beasts, over . . . children . . . there is no law."[2] He maintained that children have neither natural rights nor rights by social contract because they lack the ability to make covenants with the other members of society and to understand the consequences of such covenants. According to Hobbes, children must acknowledge their fathers as sovereigns who have the power of

TABLE 2.1
OPINION STATEMENTS AND RESPONSES ON CONTEXTUAL
ISSUES, CONFLICTS, AND DILEMMAS

*Responses** (percentages)

SA	TA	TD	SD	*Indices and Statements* †
				Index A: Rights of Parents and Children
31.8	41.6	21.0	5.6	1. The rights of children have long been neglected in favor of parental rights.
31.9	49.5	16.3	2.3	2. Too many children have been mistreated in the name of discipline.
				Index B: State Intervention
1.9	5.4	29.5	63.3	3. Public agencies should stay out of relations between parents and their children.
				Index C: Decision Criteria
16.8	52.4	24.9	5.8	4. It's difficult to say what is and what is not child mistreatment.
13.0	66.1	18.3	2.7	5. It's difficult to determine when parents should have their children returned.
				Index D: Effectiveness of Technology
7.0	29.1	49.0	14.8	6. Treatment for parents who mistreat their children is largely ineffectual.
7.1	31.9	40.7	20.3	7. We just don't know enough to deal effectively with problems of child mistreatment.
				Index E: Punitive Versus Therapeutic Orientation
57.2	36.6	4.7	1.5	8. It is therapy that parents need, not punishment.
5.8	19.9	48.9	25.4.	9. People who mistreat their children should have their parental rights terminated.
29.2	60.8	9.1	0.9	10. Parents who mistreat their children are sick, not criminals.
				Index F: Conflicts Between Punitive and Therapeutic Approaches
1.5	6.3	49.3	42.9	11. Conflicts between therapeutic services and law enforcement activities cannot be reconciled.
8.1	18.6	46.8	26.5	12. In dealing with child mistreatment, law enforcement efforts should not be mixed with service programs.
				Index G: Role Conflict
4.7	25.9	43.9	25.4	13. Physicians who are known to report cases of mistreatment of children lose the confidence of their patients.

* SA = Strongly agree, TA = Tend to agree, TD = Tend to disagree, SD = Strongly disagree
† These statements were not presented to the respondents in this order, and the interview schedule included opinion statements other than these.

life and death over them, and "every man is supposed to promise obedience to him in whose power it is to save or destroy him."[3] The rights of biological parents to custody over their children were well embedded in common law. In this country apprenticeship, the colonial response to pauper, illegitimate, or orphaned children, was partly based on the belief that "all people should be attached to a family."[4]

"With the advent of the concept *parens patrae,* it was held in English Law that the king was the . . . father of all."[5] Under this doctrine, which became part of early American common law, the state could intervene in parent-child relations when conditions warranted the protection of children. This principle has evolved into the form of *in loco parentis,* "wherein the state may stand in the place of the parent," at times assuming the custody of children through its administrative and service organizations and programs.[6]

Opinions vary in regard to the extent and impact of state intervention. Sanford H. Katz concluded, for example, that

> when one observes the expanding power of government into the family sphere, one must begin to readjust one's legal concept of family relationship, especially that of parents and child. It is not accurate to portray the parent-child relationship as one of the most jealously guarded in society—a frequently stated myth. Indeed, the greatest inroad the government has made in the family setting has been in the parent-child relationship. . . . The point is that no longer is it possible to delineate sharply the jurisdictional lines between government, parents, and children.[7]

Yet, after an examination of relevant decisions, H. H. Foster, Jr. and D. J. Freed asserted in 1972 that "sweeping declarations aside, there is a paucity of legal authority for the general proposition that children are persons under the law."[8] In 1973 another analyst observed that the thrust of most reform had been to persuade parents to treat children better, but that reform "has not changed the position of children within society or made them capable of securing such treatment for themselves."[9] Interestingly enough, some have come to view child labor legislation as a protection for adults against work displacement and devaluation of the price of labor, as much as a manifestation of concern over securing opportunities for children's education.[10]

In spite of differences over the status of children's legal rights and the impact of state intervention, most analysts agree that modification of strict paternalism has been slow and fraught with dilemmas. Among the factors contributing to the slow rate of change are: emphasis on the preservation of the family, with no appropriate substitute in sight; fear of the consequences of legal intrusion upon the authority structure within the family, and uncertainty about the secondary effects of such intrusion upon the welfare of children themselves; reluctance based upon this fear and reinforced by the relatively low incidence of reported cases of maltreatment, with maltreatment still considered by many to be exceptional; difficulties in articulating appropriate laws for regulating parent-child relations, and anticipated difficulties in enforcing such laws if enacted, especially in regard to children so young that they can neither define problems nor assess motives; "the limitations on state control of private conduct are transformed into parental control in a kind of mirror image; to the extent that the state may not interfere in some sort of conduct, it often may not interfere with parental regulation of that sort of conduct in children"; [11] and the widely held opinion that the problem cannot be addressed primarily through legal means, but falls equally within the domains of agencies offering health care, social services, and education.

Underlying much uncertainty about the role of the state in parent-child relations is the fact that "nowhere in American law is there a comprehensive statement that adequately describes the full range of the legal responsibilities of parents to children." [12] Katz attempts to develop some norms, contending that, in return for the right to secure and stable parent-child relations free from unreasonable interference, parents are expected to provide for their children's financial security, health, education, and morality; to teach them respect for authority and for others; and to provide an environment conducive to the development of sound character. [13] The literature shows other attempts toward clarifying these rights and obligations. Important among these are Alfred Kadushin's specifications of the reciprocal roles of children, parents, and the community. [14]

Statutes may refer to optimal and desirable conditions; their enforcement, however, is generally based upon identifying minimum standards below which the children's health and well-being are considered endangered. Proper administration of programs on child mal-treatment thus requires not only the clarification of parental responsibilities, but also those of the state. In this respect, Sussman and Cohen point out that

> the degree to which the state is permitted to interfere with the traditional right of the parent to guide the physical and emotional development of his child should be contingent upon the nature of the harm society and the legislature wish to prevent and the ability of the state to correct that harm. Statutes which authorize the conditions, methods, and extent of state interference into the privacy of the family should therefore be written with careful and constant reference to the purposes which legitimize such intervention.[15]

Index A in Table 2.2 assesses the positions of respondents on the rights of parents and of children. A majority, ranging from a low of 53.1 percent for the police to a high of 76.7 percent for child protective agencies, strongly felt that children's rights have not been receiving appropriate emphasis. Though expressed infrequently by all respondents (11 percent), the opposite opinions were most prevalent among respondents from the police, courts, and hospital medical departments, in that order. Index B in Table 2.2 is based upon responses to the statement, "Public agencies should stay out of the relations between parents and their children." As the distributions in the table show, the overwhelming majority of respondents reacted negatively to this statement; they did not see parent-child relations as exempt from state intervention. As will be seen later, however, there were greater differences over the forms such intervention should take.

The respondents' positions concerning these issues were found to relate to several attributes. Persons who felt the rights of children were neglected and who expressed no aversion to the intervention of public agencies tended more often to be females, in higher levels of education, older, nonmarried, with no children, working in communities reporting the existence of interagency teams, liaisons, or other forms of coordination. These respondents were also more likely to have shown interest in the study and to have been cooperative during the interviews.

TABLE 2.2
RESPONDENTS' OPINIONS ON CONTEXTUAL ISSUES, CONFLICTS, AND DILEMMAS

Organizations and Responses

Indices	CPS	PHN	SCH	HMD	HSS	CRT	POL	Total
A. Rights of Parents and Children								
Parent-oriented	6.2	5.3	7.2	15.0	5.2	18.0	18.5	11.0
Medium position	17.1	21.2	22.8	26.6	20.8	27.7	28.4	23.6
Child-oriented	76.7	73.4	70.0	58.4	74.0	54.3	53.1	65.4
B. State Intervention								
Support	96.6	93.3	93.4	90.2	95.6	89.7	89.3	92.5
Oppose	3.4	6.7	6.6	9.8	4.4	10.3	10.7	7.5
C. Decision Criteria								
Clear, specific	20.7	10.9	6.4	5.0	10.4	13.0	10.7	11.1
Medium position	35.7	25.5	25.7	30.9	26.3	35.3	33.6	30.6
Diffuse, ambiguous	43.5	63.6	67.9	64.1	63.4	51.6	55.7	58.2
D. Effectiveness of Technology								
Effective	57.4	35.8	44.6	40.5	47.2	43.4	22.1	41.3
Medium position	26.5	49.1	37.4	38.3	34.3	34.8	43.3	37.8
Not effective	16.1	15.1	17.9	21.2	18.5	21.8	34.6	20.9
E. Punitive Versus Therapeutic Orientation								
Punitive orientation	0.0	0.0	0.1	0.0	0.3	1.7	5.1	1.1
Medium position	8.2	9.9	23.4	20.5	16.7	28.2	50.2	22.7
Therapeutic orientation	91.8	90.1	76.4	79.5	83.0	70.0	44.7	76.2
F. Conflicts Between Punitive and Therapeutic Approaches								
Reconcilable	58.2	64.4	79.7	65.0	62.2	70.3	76.0	68.3
Medium position	35.7	34.3	18.5	28.8	32.2	26.5	18.2	27.5
Irreconcilable	6.1	1.3	1.8	6.1	5.7	3.2	5.8	4.2
G. Role Conflict								
High	22.9	41.2	47.4	30.4	26.2	31.3	32.8	33.4
Low	77.1	58.8	52.6	69.6	73.8	68.7	67.2	66.6

STATUS OF KNOWLEDGE AND TECHNOLOGY

The status of knowledge and technology concerning child abuse and neglect poses many difficulties. The lack of epidemiological knowledge, for example, has been a major factor in retarding preventive efforts. More will be said about this at a later point in the report. Two other issues concerning knowledge and technology in this field are particularly significant to the purposes of this work. The first is the vagueness of the criteria for abusive or negligent acts. The second is the adequacy of available knowledge and technology.

Criteria for Identification and Decision

Cases close to the two ends of any continuum are readily identifiable; toward the middle of the continuum, however, there is always a doubtful area. The area of doubt seems especially large in regard to cases of child abuse and neglect. At the heart of the problem lies the question of when and in what forms maltreatment is to be considered disciplinary, excessive, or abusive. Much has been written about this question, ranging from societal prescriptions denouncing violence to specific justifications for court rulings. Nevertheless, the numerous statements made about the subject thus far have neither significantly clarified the criteria nor narrowed the range of doubtful cases.

The two sides of this issue are reflected in the language of an 1840 court ruling on a case of "excessive punishment" and in a statement on children's rights made in a 1970 report to the President by the White House Conference on Children. The court ruled that

> the right of parents to chastise their refractory and disobedient children is so necessary to the government of families, to the good order of society, that no moralist or lawgiver has ever thought of interferring with its existence, or of calling upon them to account for the manner of its exercise, upon light or frivolous pretenses. But, at the same time that the law has created and preserved this right, in its regard for the safety of the child it has prescribed bounds beyond which it shall not be carried.
> In chastising a child, the parent must be careful that he does not exceed the bounds of moderation and inflict cruel and merciless punishment; if he does, he is a trespasser, and liable to be punished by indictment. It is not, then, the infliction of punishment, but the excess, which constitutes the offense, and what this excess shall be is not a conclusion of law, but a question of fact for the determination of the jury.[16]

The White House Conference on Children confirmed a commitment to children's rights to optimal health, growth and development, and to security—which was further specified as

> an absence of want; it also includes a sense of future security—an absence of fear of the future, a sense of the regularity of basic necessities defined in the context of a society with material abundance, and a sense of control over important life choices. When such security cannot be afforded by parents alone, society must provide the means for achieving it; at the same time society must preserve the family's dignity and its right to decision making.[17]

Although perhaps helping to sensitize the reader to general conditions and forms of behavior, terms like "refractory and disobedient," "cruel and merciless," "excess," "optimal health and development," "security," and "family's dignity," do not lead to specific criteria, especially for cases toward the middle of the continuum. This lack of clear and objective criteria reflects fundamental limitations in the state of knowledge about child development; it constitutes the most difficult obstacle to appropriate decision-making in connection with child maltreatment.

The reactions of respondents attest to the ambiguity and vagueness of current criteria. As the distributions on Index C (Table 2.2) indicate, only small minorities of the weighted responses, ranging from 5 percent for hospital medical departments to 20.7 percent for child protective services, considered available criteria sufficiently specific and clear. Conversely, much greater proportions of these responses, ranging from a high of 67.9 percent for respondents from school systems to a low of 43.5 percent for those from child protective agencies, found decision criteria badly lacking in specificity and clarity. It is interesting that physicians, whose work is based on the more difficult and advanced technologies, expressed much greater skepticism about the current status of decision criteria than did respondents from child protective services.

Respondents' evaluation of criteria exhibited a weak relationship to community size and to the number of reported cases of abuse and neglect: the larger the community size and the number of cases, the greater the tendency to view the criteria as clear and unambiguous. The existence of interagency teams and liaison activities was also associated with positive assessments of available criteria. These relationships might have suggested the respondents' level of education as the underlying link, since higher levels were more characteristic of larger communities, as were teams and liaisons. The relations between the educational levels of respondents and their assessment of criteria, however, followed a somewhat curvilinear pattern. Respondents in the highest and lowest levels of education were similar in viewing the decision criteria as diffuse and ambiguous, with those in the middle educational levels reporting fewer problems with criteria. None of the other attributes of the respondents were related to this index in a consistent manner.

Adequacy of Knowledge and Technology

The second issue concerns the adequacy and effectiveness of available knowledge and technology. Technologies determine the means available for reaching the goals of agencies and programs.[18] Of the different fields involved in the problems of abuse and neglect, certain areas of medicine stand out as the most technologically advanced. The knowledge and skills of pediatricians, radiologists, and surgeons in diagnosing and treating victimized children constitute impressive coping capabilities. Unfortunately, the complexity of the problem goes beyond the diagnosis and treatment of physical problems. It entails identifying and treating whatever emotional damage the children might have sustained, motivating parents and others to report cases of suspected abuse, changing the behavior of abusive parents and guardians in order to prevent repetition, deciding when children should and should not be left with their families, and collecting legally admissible evidence for protecting the rights of children.

Technologies for achieving these latter objectives are seriously underdeveloped. Consider counseling, for example. There is no reason to believe that counseling has firmer technological foundations than those of psychiatry, which has been described as not offering a viable technology.[19] The literature includes conflicting evaluations of various approaches, both in changing the abusive behavior of parents and in dealing with their related emotional problems. While social welfare agencies continue their professional approach to the problem, some consider nonprofessional help more effective; others find greater assistance in organizations of parents experiencing similar problems (Parents Anonymous) modeled after such groups as Alcoholics Anonymous.[20]

The level of technological development offers a useful insight into the structure and performance of service and law enforcement organizations. Developed technologies lead to a greater articulation of roles in the structure of organizations, less subjectivity in decisions and operations, more identifiable outcomes, and greater specificity in criteria for assessing these outcomes. Index D (Table 2.2) presents respondents' opinions about the effectiveness of available technology, based on their reactions to the following two statements: "We just don't know enough to deal effectively with problems of child mistreatment," and "Treatment for parents who mistreat their children is largely ineffectual."

The reactions of respondents varied widely. High opinions of the effectiveness of current intervention techniques were expressed in weighted responses ranging from a high of 57.4 percent for child protective agencies to a low of 22.1 percent for the police. Negative assessments ranged from 34.6 percent for the police to 15.1 percent for public health departments. Considering the strength of the two statements, and the fact that the respondents are likely to have direct experience of the available technological developments, the distribution of responses is not reassuring.

Positive assessments of effectiveness tended to come from respondents in larger communities or from those reporting higher numbers of abuse and neglect cases. More women than men believed available technology was highly effective. Once again, however, educational levels showed a curvilinear relation to these assessments. More of the weighted responses among persons with the highest and the lowest educational attainments questioned the effectiveness of technological developments in the field, while respondents in the middle levels viewed such developments more positively. Does this pattern reaffirm the adage about the dangers of "a little learning"?

PUNITIVE AND THERAPEUTIC APPROACHES

One of the most significant policy and program dilemmas concerning child maltreatment arises from the difficulty of deciding between therapeutic and punitive approaches, particularly toward neglectful and abusive parents and guardians. During the last quarter of the nineteenth century organizations concerned with the prevention of cruelty to children improved the therapeutic milieu for affected children; the approach of these organizations to abusers, however, was strictly punitive. Convinced that cruel and irresponsible parents or guardians deserved to be punished, and that punishment could serve as a deterrent to the initiation or repetition of abusive acts, these institutions pursued abusers into the courts.

More recently, significantly different interpretations of deviant acts such as child abuse and neglect have been introduced. Individual responsibility, upon which punitive approaches were predicated, yielded to interpretations involving mental and emotional conditions beyond the individual's control. Also, greater weight was assigned to environmental factors in the precipitation of these acts. These interpretations and analyses lessen the weight of responsibility and blame attributed to abusers, who had previously been considered completely willful and fully aware of the consequences of their acts. Rather than deserving punishment, abusers have come to be regarded as patients needing treatment and help with their health problems or with environmental stresses. Besides, most victimized children are either left with their parents or are eventually returned to them; this fact alone adds considerable strength to the justification for therapeutic approaches to the problem.

Although current attitudes are less punitive than earlier ones, emphasizing the protection of children rather than the prosecution of abusive and neglectful parents and guardians, the punitive-therapeutic dilemma remains significant in the structure and provision of services. No matter how the intervention of public agencies is perceived and defined by their personnel, most parents are unlikely to view police or social services investigations, court hearings, and custody challenges over their children to be anything but punitive.

Statements constituting Index E (Table 2.1), which assesses positions on this dilemma, were phrased in a way that openly polarizes the two alternatives. The distribution of weighted responses (Table 2.2) shows that espousal of the strongest therapeutic orientation ranged from a high of 91.8 percent for respondents from child protection agencies to a low of 44.7 percent for those from the police. Very few, mostly respondents from the police and the courts, were willing to characterize as criminals parents who mistreat their children and very few saw them as deserving punishment rather than therapy. Nevertheless, sizable proportions of the weighted responses were in a middle position.

Differences in orientation between law enforcement agencies (the police and the courts) and social and health services are clearly reflected in the patterns of reactions to the index statements. Equally important are differences within each group of respondents. A therapeutic orientation was more likely to be characteristic of women, of persons with higher educational attainments, and of those in communities with developed interagency teams or other forms of coordination.

The issue of therapy versus punishment was further pursued in this study by seeking the respondents' assessments of the reconcilability of the two approaches. Index F (Table 2.2) measures the reactions of respondents in this respect. The majority of the weighted responses indicated that the two orientations are reconcilable. It is interesting to note that respondents from the police and the courts were more likely than those from child protective agencies to view differences as reconcilable. Though expressed infrequently by all respondents (4.2 percent), the opposite position was most prevalent among protective agencies and the police. Equally important are the sizable proportions of respondents from all agencies who took a middle position in their assessment of the potential for bridging the gaps between punitive and therapeutic approaches. There were no strong patterns of association between positions on this index and respondents' attributes, except that optimistic views about reconciling these conflicts were more characteristic of men than women, and of respondents from communities where teams and other interagency liaisons existed. Also, those who held these views were more cooperative during the interviews.

ROLE CONFLICTS

When the punitive and therapeutic approaches are combined in the same role set, conflicts in roles can ensue. Physicians encounter this conflict when required by law to report suspected cases of abuse among people in their care, as do caseworkers when obliged to initiate legal proceedings against parents to whom they are also expected to extend counseling and other services. At issue is the relationship of trust and openness to the demands of effective therapy; the need for trust and openness between doctors and patients is undoubtedly one of the reasons for the AMA's opposition to statutes requiring physicians' reporting. It should be noted that the mere possibility that therapists might initiate or participate in punitive proceedings is sufficient to affect adversely the establishment of appropriate therapeutic relationships with parents. The impairment of such relationships assumes greater significance in view of the fact that parents and guardians are not only the sources of information about themselves, but also often the sources of information about the children. This role conflict has serious implications for case identification, for the likelihood of services being sought for affected children, for the response of parents to therapy, and for relations among agencies.

Index G (Table 2.2) represents reactions to the statement "Physicians who are known to report cases of mistreatment of children lose the confidence of their patients." Although a majority of the weighted responses from each group gave negative reactions to this statement, the proportions in agreement were sizable, ranging from a high of 47.4 percent for respondents from school systems to a low of 22.9 percent for those from child protective services. Of particular importance are responses from hospital medical personnel, 30.4 percent of whom affirmed the reality of this conflict. Also to be noted are the affirmative responses of personnel from public health services (41.2 percent) and those from hospital social services (26.2 percent). These two groups of respondents can be expected to be fairly accurate in their assessment of the existence of such role conflicts among independent practitioners and hospital-based physicians. Finally, the smaller the size of the community, the greater the likelihood that respondents would have perceived role conflicts among physicians required to report suspected child maltreatment by their patients. This is consistent with the anonymity and diminished emphasis upon informal relations in larger communities.

Conflicts within the role sets of certain personnel in the field also arise when their positions entail responsibility for the welfare of clients whose interests are not always compatible. Caseworkers in child protective services often find themselves caught in this form of conflict because they represent the interests of both abused and neglected children and of abusive and neglectful parents and guardians. A common criticism leveled against these agencies' practices is that caseworkers either identify with the children to the point of antagonism toward parents, or with the parents to the point of endangering the safety of children.[21] Conflicts in caseworkers' roles are further compounded when they become simultaneously involved with a third group of clients, foster parents, and especially with those who are potential adopters. Although their positions illustrate these conflicts most clearly, caseworkers are not unique in experiencing such conflicts.

ORGANIZATIONAL AND PROFESSIONAL DOMAINS

The multidimensional nature of the problem of child maltreatment necessitates the involvement of a number of independent agencies and a variety of professions. Several public agencies, whose domains include responsibilities toward the prevention and control of these problems, have already been identified. In addition, there are numerous voluntary organizations in the field. As Martin Rein has observed, social services are in many ways the last bastion of free enterprise; any time two people come together in the name of good works, they can start a service agency.[22] "They can even claim to be coordinating the work of other agencies who, in turn, have the right to ignore them."[23] Involvement in abuse and neglect programs extends beyond public and voluntary agencies to include individual physicians and other clinicians who encounter the problem in private practice and who are often required to report suspected cases to appropriate authorities.

This multiorganizational and multiprofessional involvement makes it informative to view new program developments in the field from interorganizational and interprofessional perspectives; this inevitably raises the issue of "domains." Warren's conception of organizational domain, applicable also to professions, is helpful analytically: "organizational domain is the organization's locus in the interorganizational network, including its legitimized 'right' to operate in specific geographic and functional areas and its channels of access to task and maintenance resources. The two important components here are the organization's right to do something, and its access to the resources it needs in order to do it."[24] In this sense, the domains of the organizations and professions involved with child maltreatment can be defined in terms of the legitimized rights of access to populations of children at risk, abused and neglected children, and/or potential and actual perpetrators; specialization in areas of knowledge, techniques, and a sphere of functional activities appropriate to the tasks of control and treatment of the problem; and access to manpower, technological means, facilities, and other resources to maintain the organizational and professional concerns themselves and to enable them to address these tasks. Often, unfortunately, maintaining and enhancing organizational and professional concerns supersedes interest in the populations served and in effective control and treatment programs.

The relations among organizations and professions can be seen in large part as the management of domains and the articulation of boundaries. Several explanations have been advanced to characterize these relations, and especially to account for the interaction among organizations. Important among these explanations is one that postulates a tendency for organizations to protect and expand their domains.[25] This proposition sheds light on competition among organizations and professions, especially when access to new or additional resources is at stake.

Such competition was experienced, covertly and overtly, by many communities attempting to respond to the problems of child maltreatment by selecting organizations to seek demonstration grants and to coordinate activities for the demonstrations. The tendency toward expanding domains was manifested also in many demonstration proposals, in which applicant organizations emphasized the creation of new services under their control, rather than further development of and closer working relations with agencies already offering these services. Thus, for example, the plans of an applicant hospital were more likely to call for developing a new child mental health clinic within its own structure than for sharing resources with an independent clinic in the community. Similarly, the plans of an applicant mental health clinic were more likely to call for adding social workers to the clinic's staff to work with the families involved than for sharing resources with existing social and protective services. This form of organizational behavior is not unique to hospitals or clinics. The attempts here are not merely to expand domains, but to expand them in ways that would assure control over wider aspects of the "task environment."

While the expansion of domains might account for the behavior of some organizations involved in coping with child maltreatment, it cannot explain the tendency on the part of others either to resist participation or to do so only reluctantly. The schools, for instance, a natural place for early detection and successful intervention, have a much lower record of reporting suspected cases and of contributing to control programs than would have been expected. The same can be said about the frequent failure of offices of prosecuting attorneys to provide adequate legal support to child protection agencies.

An understanding of the motives and conditions behind negative organizational behavior is needed in order to create incentives and conditions that will assure more effective participation. To consider negative organizational behavior as simply a resistance to expansion would be mistaken, for these organizations strive to expand in other directions. Instructional programs are expanded in schools, criminal justice is expanded in the activities of prosecuting attorneys. Rather, the explanation lies in the allocation of priorities according to the functions to be added, and the potential of those functions for a corresponding increase in resources. With the exception of family and juvenile courts, pediatric services in hospitals, and child protection agencies, other organizations in this study are preoccupied largely with objectives different from or much broader than the control of child abuse and neglect. The performance of these latter organizations is not judged by their contributions to the control of this problem, nor is their involvement likely to enhance their access to resources commensurate with the efforts required.

Three approaches suggest themselves in dealing with this problem: to motivate agencies to undertake certain activities through an increase in resources, appropriate recognition of efforts and results, and other types of incentives; to mandate legally that certain functions and tasks be performed by given agencies, thus setting statutory boundaries for their responsibility toward the problem; or to increase awareness about the respective roles they can constructively perform through educational programs within and outside the agencies. Undoubtedly, the solution lies more in a mix of all three approaches than in emphasis upon any one.

Two conditions sap the effectiveness of these approaches in resolving the articulation of agency boundaries. First, some organizations and professions might view involvement as at least controversial or, worse yet, as conflicting with their primary objectives. The second condition involves the ambiguity that surrounds definitions, criteria, and approaches to the problem, an ambiguity that has been reflected all along in uncertain jurisdictional boundaries and unclear divisions of responsibility among agencies.

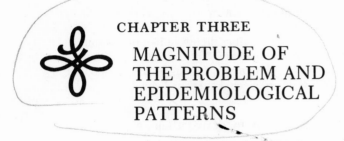

CHAPTER THREE

MAGNITUDE OF THE PROBLEM AND EPIDEMIOLOGICAL PATTERNS

ACCURATE ASSESSMENTS of the magnitude of the problem of child maltreatment and its dimensions in the various communities would provide a rational basis both for the distribution of resources among agencies and programs and for a meaningful evaluation of their performance. To account for the "true" incidence of abuse and neglect, however, is more an ideal than an attainable goal. Still, an ideal goal serves the important function of indicating ways to improve attainable approximations. Available national estimates of the number of cases of abuse and neglect vary widely. In the following passages, which we quote at length, Alan Sussman and Stephan J. Cohen detail some of the important variations:

The most commonly quoted national figure is that of 60,000 incidents each year, but what this number denotes is subject to wide interpretation. Senator Mondale, in his opening remarks before the Subcommittee hearings on the Child Abuse Prevention Act of 1973, stated, "Each year, some 60,000 children in this country are *reported* to have been abused." The Education Commission of the States reports the same figure, but claims that 60,000 children are actually *physically* abused each year. . . .

. . . David Gil, citing data from a 1965 National Opinion Research Center survey of public attitudes and opinions about physical abuse, estimated that "the figures 2.53 and 4.07 millions, respectively, would represent . . . the lower and upper limits of the annual nationwide incidence of child abuse resulting in some injury. . . ." Due to some limitations of the NORC study, however, Gil added that the actual incidence rate "was not determined by the survey, and is likely to be considerably lower."

Using Gil's NORC data, but making slightly different assumptions, Richard Light estimates that between 200,000 and 500,000 children are physically abused each year. Additionally, he suggests that 465,000 to 1,170,000 children are severely neglected or sexually molested each year in America.[1]

Sussman and Cohen went on to derive their own national estimates based on the reported incidence of abuse and neglect in the ten most populated states, which include about one-half of the U.S. population, and the confirmation rates of reports in eight states where such records were maintained.[2] Their projections for 1972 and 1973, respectively, yielded 35,267 and 38,779 confirmed cases of abuse figures which they considered to be the "uppermost permissible estimates" from the data available to them.[3] Sussman and Cohen further qualified their findings, noting that the current status of reporting suffers many limitations. Important among these are differences in the statutory definitions of abuse and neglect, in the ages of children covered by the laws, and in the types of cases for which reporting is mandated; diffuseness in identifying criteria; reluctance on the part of many laymen and professionals to report cases they suspect; and the wide discretion officials who receive the reports have in decisions concerning record keeping and confirmation.

Although aware of these and other shortcomings in the reporting and registering of abuse and neglect, we still felt that an account of the number of reported cases in jurisdictions included in this survey would be informative, and furthermore, that projections of these figures to the national population would provide useful approximations of the magnitude of the problem in the United States. Three estimates were computed in this analysis of the national incidence of abuse and neglect during the year 1972. These estimates were based upon rates in all sampling jurisdictions in this survey; rates in the state of Florida; and rates in the high-reporting jurisdictions in the survey sample. Data on reporting and confirmation rates in the sample jurisdictions were also used in projections to arrive at estimates of the rates of confirmable abuse and neglect, under existing laws and practices, and estimates of the probabilities of confirmation of reports at varying levels of reporting. This chapter presents the rationale for the assumptions, data elements, computational procedures, and results of these estimates and projections.

Before turning to these estimates, however, it is important to clarify the types and meaning of rates in this analysis. Distinctions need to be made between three types of rates. First, there are incidence rates of maltreatment, constituting the number of new cases that occur during a specified period of time in relation to a given population at the midpoint of that period. A specification of these rates requires knowledge of the time of onset of maltreatment and whether the rates are of episodes or of a pattern of maltreatment. Second, there are prevalence rates, referring to the proportions of victims of maltreatment in a given population at any given time in relation to that population. The third type of rates might be termed incidence of reporting; this rate comprises the number of cases reported during a period of time in relation to a given population at the midpoint of that period. Discussion in the literature on child maltreatment often confuses these three types of rates. Because of the chronic nature of much abuse and neglect, we believe the term *prevalence* is more applicable than *incidence* to current data in the literature. In this presentation, *incidence* is used to designate incidence of reporting, rather than of maltreatment. Exceptions will be found in quotations from or references to the work of others where the term *incidence* was used indiscriminately.

ESTIMATES

Overall Estimates

Information was sought from each of the various agencies and respondents covered in this study about the number of abuse and neglect reports or referrals. Since reports from agencies serving the same populations were expected to entail considerable overlap, it was necessary to decide which responses were to be used in estimating incidence rates for the sampling jurisdictions and in projecting estimates to the nation. Controversy over the designation of agencies as recipients of abuse and neglect reports generally centered around the availability and merits of social service agencies as against those of police departments.[4]

For several reasons, incidence estimates from this survey are based on responses from child protection agencies. By 1973, the trend among the states was toward naming child protection agencies either exclusively or in combination with other agencies to receive reports of abuse and neglect. Furthermore, protection agencies are the only organizations whose mission is totally addressed to this problem. These factors alone would have been sufficient to weight the decision in favor of using responses from these agencies for estimating incidence. The sampling plans however, also made it necessary to rely on data from child protective agencies. These data were the most appropriate for national projections since the jurisdictions of the agencies are coterminous with population reporting units of the U.S. Census.

Questions about the experiences of agencies with the magnitude of the problem elicited data on:

The number of cases (children under 18) of abuse and neglect referred or reported to the agency or identified by its personnel during the last year, prior to interviews, for which figures were available;

Definitions of the years for which figures were available;

The proportions of cases considered abuse and those considered neglect;

The proportions of reports of suspected abuse and of suspected neglect that were subsequently confirmed.

Often, interviewers made second visits to obtain figures related to these questions, and they often obtained copies of the agencies' statistical reports or records. It should be noted that interviews were conducted in 129 of the 130 counties and equivalent jurisdictions in which the survey sample was located. Of these 129, data on reported cases were obtained from 116.

These new figures were utilized in computing the incidence for the sample jurisdictions and making national projections based on the weighting framework described in Chapter 1. The 13 counties which failed to provide data on the reported incidence of abuse and neglect were assigned the average weighted rates of the 116 that provided such information. As pointed out earlier, incidence rates of reporting represent the numbers of new reports that occur during a specified period of time, divided by the reference population at the midpoint of that period. Because of the many crudities characteristic of available data on reports of abuse and neglect, however, it was believed unnecessary to make specific population projections for the various sampling jurisdictions for the midpoints of the years represented by the incidence data provided. Instead, it was decided to rely on population figures from the 1970 U.S. Census updated to reflect 1972.

The first two columns in Table 3.1 show estimates for the sampling jurisdictions and projections to the U.S. population along several dimensions of the problem. The national projections in the second column were based on the weighted incidence of reported abuse and neglect in the sample areas; this rate was 8.78 per 1,000 children under 18 years of age. This means that 611,684 children in these age categories were reported as suspected victims to protective services throughout the country during 1972. Of these, 27.3 percent (166,702) were considered by these agencies to be cases of abuse; the remaining 72.7 percent (444,982) were considered cases of neglect. Of the reported abuse cases 71.3 percent were confirmed, as were 69.6 percent of the reported neglect cases.

Projecting these proportions to the U.S. population would lead to estimates of 118,794 confirmed cases of abuse and 309,592 confirmed cases of neglect. In other words, for every 1,000 children under 18 in the country, 1.71 cases of abuse and 4.45 of neglect were suspected, brought to the attention of protective services, and confirmed. Because of inadequacies in reporting, to be more fully discussed at a later point, the numbers of cases and rates of incidence presented above constitute the lowest of the estimates prepared for this analysis.

Estimates Based on Florida Incidence

Whenever the issue of a standard for case identification and reporting is discussed, the state of Florida comes to mind. As mentioned earlier, changes in the statutes which govern the reporting of abuse and neglect, as well as the implementation of statewide WATS lines, backed by an effective campaign of public information, raised the number of cases reported in one year (1970 to 1971) from 17 to 19, 120. From October 1972 through September 1973—the year that most closely represents the period for which figures were obtained from most of the agencies in this survey—the frequency of such reports had stabilized, reaching 29,013 for children under 17—the age limit for which reporting was required by law in that state.

Aside from these statutory age limitations, there were no special reasons to believe that reporting in Florida would have been different for 17-year-old children than it was for the 16-year-olds (1,115 persons). Therefore, it was estimated that 30,099 cases would have been reported in Florida during that year if the ages of children for whom reporting was required had included the 17-year-olds. In 1972 the population of children under the age of 18 in Florida was estimated at about 2,118,000.[5] When the rates of reporting are related to this population, the yield is an incidence rate of approximately 14.21 reported cases per 1,000 children. Should all parts of the nation have had a level of reporting similar to that of Florida, 1,000,420 reports of suspected cases would have come to the attention of public authorities (Table 3.1).

No precise distinctions are made in the Florida data between abuse and neglect. Nevertheless, on the basis of the acts of maltreatment committed, Polansky and his associates attempted to classify the cases into these two categories.[6] The results of their efforts led to a ratio of 23.7 cases of abuse to 76.3 cases of neglect, which differs little from that yielded through the national survey. Applying this ratio to national projections yields 237,100 cases of suspected abuse and 763,320 of suspected neglect. Assuming that the rate of confirmation for all reported cases in the state (56 percent) applies equally to both abuse and neglect, it is possible to estimate 132,776 confirmable cases of abuse and 427,459 of neglect.[7]

If we can assume that differences between projections based on the weighted averages of the sampling jurisdictions and on reporting in Florida are due to underreporting in the former, we can compare the figures in the second and third columns of Table 3.1 for an approximation of the magnitude of underreporting. Considering the dif-

TABLE 3.1
ESTIMATES OF REPORTED INCIDENCE IN SAMPLING JURISDICTIONS,
WITH POPULATION-WIDE PROJECTIONS

Items	Estimates in Sampling Jurisdictions	Projections to the U.S. Population*		
		Based on Incidence in Weighted Averages of All Sampling Jurisdictions	Based on Incidence in Florida†	Based on Incidence in Highest Sampling Jurisdiction
Number of children* under 18 years of age	21,673,282	69,644,081	69,644,081	69,644,081
Weighted abuse and neglect incidence rates (per 1,000 children)	8.78	8.78	14.21	21.47
Numbers of reported cases	185,850	611,684	1,000,420	1,495,467
Weighted proportion of all reports considered abuse	27.3	27.3	23.7	17.0
Number of cases considered abuse	50,737	166,702	237,100	254,573
Weighted proportion of all reports considered neglect	72.7	72.7	76.3	83.0
Number of cases considered neglect	135,113	444,982	763,320	1,240,894
Weighted proportion of reported abuse confirmed	71.3	71.3	56.0	67.4
Number of cases of reported abuse confirmed	36,156	118,794	132,776	171,547
Weighted proportion of reported neglect confirmed	69.6	69.6	56.0	71.4
Number of cases of reported neglect confirmed	94,004	309,592	427,459	886,408

NOTE: For calculating numbers of cases, the rates used included three decimal digits. Therefore, differences are due to rounding off to one decimal digit.
* Based on 1970 Census.
† Rates of confirmation in Florida were 56 percent (see Sussman and Cohen, *Reporting Child Abuse and Neglect*, p. 129).

ferential rates of confirmation, such a comparison would reveal that 13,982 confirmable cases of abuse and 117,867 of neglect were unreported during the year covered in this study. For these to be identified, 388,736 more cases in the nation would have had to be brought to the attention of appropriate agencies.

Estimates Based on High-Reporting Jurisdictions

Expectations were that, with very minor exceptions, the rates of reporting in Florida (14.21 per 1,000 children under 18) would have far exceeded those of all jurisdictions in the sample. Responses in the survey indicate, however, that the rates of reported incidence of abuse and neglect in the sampling jurisdictions ranged from 0.25 to 59.62 per 1,000. Furthermore, of the 129 agencies participating in the study, 21 (representing 21.7 percent of the population) had actually reported higher rates of incidence than those of Florida. Utilizing data from these 21 jurisdictions, a third set of national projections was prepared, as shown in the fourth column of Table 3.1. These projections constitute the upper limits of estimates for the magnitude of the problem that can be derived from our data. It might be argued that an average of the highest 10 percent, or even a more restricted portion of the range of rates, would have been a better estimator of the upper limits. There are no specific rules for selecting among alternative cutting points on a continuum of this type. In order to allow for greater stability in estimates, preference was given in these computations to including all jurisdictions that exceeded Florida. Naturally, this position yields more conservative projections.

As shown in Table 3.1, the average weighted rate of reporting for the "highest jurisdictions" was 21.47 per 1,000 children under 18 years of age. Of these cases, 17 percent were considered abuse and the remaining 83 percent neglect. The rates of confirmation for high-reporting jurisdictions varied little from those for the total sample. Projecting these rates to the U.S. population of children under 18 would indicate that a much larger portion of the problem remains unidentified. These projections (last column in Table 3.1) show that during that year there would have been 171,547 confirmable cases of abuse or 886,408 of neglect in the nation; these confirmable cases would have resulted from 254,573 and 1,240,894 reports of suspected cases, respectively.

Considering the possibility that figures from the high-reporting sample jurisdictions constitute closer approximations of the "true" incidence, and considering the differential rates of confirmation, it can be said that 52,753 confirmable cases of abuse and 576,816 cases of neglect failed to be reported during the year covered in the survey. To have reached these cases would have required the reporting of 87,871 more suspected abuse cases and 795,912 suspected neglect cases during the year.

Estimates Based on Projections of Reporting and Confirmation Rates

The relations among the rates of reporting of abuse and neglect, the rates of confirmed abuse in the population, and the estimated probability that a case will or will not be confirmed exhibited important patterns. As the rates of reporting increased, the rates of confirmed maltreatment increased rapidly up to a certain point, after which the rate of increase tended to lessen considerably (see the solid part of the curve in Figure 3.1). The relations between the rates of reporting and the estimated probability that maltreatment cases will be confirmed, however, exhibited the reverse pattern: the probability of confirming reports of suspected cases dropped sharply as the rates of reporting increased. The curves representing data collected in this study are shown in Figure 3.2. The behavior of these two curves enabled us, through projections based on available data, to obtain three crucial estimates: the rates of confirmable abuse and neglect in the nation under current laws and practices; the rates of reporting needed to uncover given proportions of confirmable maltreatment; and the probability of confirmation at varying levels of reporting and at varying proportions of known abuse and neglect.

Estimates of the national rates of confirmable abuse were obtained by projecting the curve relating the rates of reporting to those of identified and confirmed abuse to the maximum where all children under 18 would have been reported (Figure 3.1). (To spare the reader the complex technical procedures involved in this projection,

FIGURE 3.1

THE RELATIONS BETWEEN RATES OF REPORTING AND RATES
OF CONFIRMABLE PREVALENCE OF CHILD MALTREATMENT

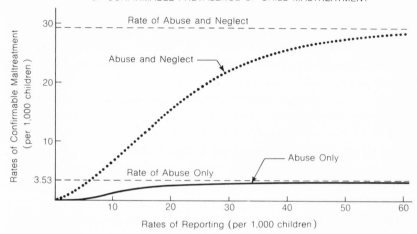

Rates of Reporting (per 1,000 children)

this information has been placed in a reference.)[8] The projections yielded a rate of 3.53 per 1,000 (± .56) confirmable abuse cases under current laws and organizational practices. These figures indicate three projected rates of confirmable abuse for the year 1972.[9] The rates and the numbers they represent are as follows:

Low (2.97 per 1,000)	=	204,978 children
Medium (3.53 per 1,000)	=	243,626 children
High (4.09 per 1,000)	=	282,275 children

When neglect cases were added to those of abuse, the total rates of confirmable maltreatment in the nation increased dramatically. The estimates obtained for these total rates reached 29.7 per 1,000 (±2.0) for the year 1972. The rates and numbers these figures represent are:

Low (27.7 per 1,000)	=	1,911,743 children
Medium (29.7 per 1,000)	=	2,049,775 children
High (31.7 per 1,000)	=	2,187,807 children

Projections of child abuse fall within the range of Richard J. Light's estimates, which ranged from 200,000 to 500,000.[10] It should also be noted that during 1972, according to the middle projections, 51.2

percent of the confirmable abuse cases in the nation (involving 124,832 children) remained unidentified. And again, considering the middle projections for the total of child maltreatment, it can be estimated that only 20.9 percent of this total, comprising 428,386 cases, was identified and confirmed during the year of the survey.

Projections of the rates of reporting in relation to those of identified and confirmed child maltreatment (Figure 3.1) help in estimating the levels of reporting of suspected cases necessary for uncovering given proportions of confirmable cases. For example, according to these estimates, to identify 75 percent of the confirmable cases of abuse would require reporting at the rate of 20 per 1,000; to identify 90 percent of the confirmable cases would require reporting at the rate of 28 per 1,000; and for 95 percent, 34 per 1,000 would be needed. The corresponding figures for total maltreatment (abuse and neglect) are 30 per 1,000, 43 per 1,000, and 52 per 1,000.

The relations between rates of identifiable maltreatment and rates of reporting hold many implications in regard to policy and program operations. Central in this respect is the question of how much effort and cost in generating and investigating reports would be justified by the additional increments of confirmable maltreatment uncovered. Information about the severity of maltreatment and the degree of threat to victims would be very helpful in resolving this question. If the more severe cases surface earlier, then substantially increased reporting might yield increments too small to warrant serious and urgent effort. Because no data on severity were within the scope of this work, however, the issue remains open. It is one that deserves research attention.

Moving now to the third set of projections yielded through this analysis, we take up the probability that a case will or will not be confirmed at varying levels of reporting. These probabilities are referred to as "true positives" and "false positives," respectively. True positives are reported cases, found upon investigation, to actually entail child maltreatment according to prevailing laws and practices of agencies. False positives comprise reported cases which upon investigation were not found to involve maltreatment. Estimates of the "true negatives" and the "false negatives" were beyond the range of our data, since they would require the screening and investigation of

FIGURE 3.2

RATES OF REPORTING AND RATES OF CONFIRMATION

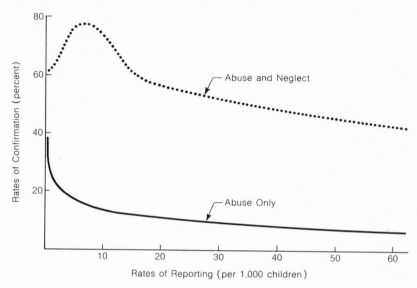

Rates of Reporting (per 1,000 children)

a random sample of nonreported children. The curves in Figure 3.2 depict the estimated relations between confirmation rates for abuse cases, for total maltreatment, and for rates of reporting. The confirmation rate for abuse cases declines rapidly as reporting increases. For example, a reporting rate of 10 per 1,000 would be associated with a confirmation rate of about 13 percent; for a reporting rate of 50 per 1,000, the confirmation rate for abuse cases would drop to about 7 percent. Projecting this trend up to the maximum point of having all children reported shows a continued decline in the rates of confirmation.[11] When reporting rates reach 100 per 1,000 and 200 per 1,000, the rates of confirmation for abuse would have decreased to 3.1 percent and 1.6 percent, respectively. The rates of confirmation for total maltreatment (abuse and neglect combined) show a similar pattern. Confirmation rates of 70 percent and 46 percent would be associated with reporting rates of 10 per 1,000 and 50 per 1,000 respectively. Projections to reporting rates of 100 and 200 per 1,000 would mean confirmation at the rates of 32 percent and 15 percent, in that order. In other words, 68 percent of those reported at rates of 100 per 1,000 and 85 percent of those reported at rates of 200 per 1,000 would have been reported, investigated, and found to entail neither abuse nor neglect as defined by current laws and organizational practices.

Equally if not more applicable to policy and program decisions and operations is the ratio of true positives to false positives, that is, the relation between the rates of known maltreatment and the probability that a given case will be confirmed. Figure 3.3 incorporates a graphic representation of this ratio, which shows a steady decline with the increase in percentages of confirmable maltreatment identified. To identify 50 percent of confirmable cases of total maltreatment, the rate of confirmation will be 54 percent—that is, false positives will have reached 44 percent of the cases reported. In other words, 44 percent of the reports will be found to be unsubstantiated. According to these projections, to identify 75 percent and 90 percent of confir-

FIGURE 3.3

PERCENTAGES OF MALTREATMENT IDENTIFIED AND
RATES OF CONFIRMATION

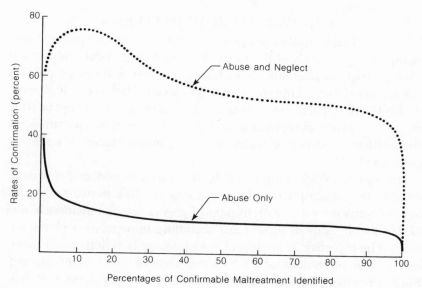

mable maltreatment cases, the rates of confirmation would be 52 percent and 46 percent, respectively—that is, the proportions of false positives will have reached 48 percent and 54 percent of the reported cases. The policy and program issues engendered by these relations concern the appropriate trade-offs between the numbers of families brought into question and subjected to investigation and the proportion of abused children who remain unidentified. Data on the distribution of severities of abuse in relation to early and later reporting would be equally useful in resolving this issue.

The estimates and figures in this analysis represent projections based on a limited range of the rates of reporting, and therefore should be interpreted with caution. Equally important, however, are the techniques used in these projections, which can be applied toward better estimates as data on reporting and rates of confirmation are improved. The same techniques can be used to arrive at estimates specific to the age of children, to their sex, to socioeconomic levels, or to any other characteristics. Should data on the severity of abuse become available, this approach to analysis would hold even greater promise for addressing crucial policy and program issues.

EPIDEMIOLOGICAL PATTERNS

Initially limited to studies of epidemics, the field of epidemiology now incorporates the study of the rates, distributions, and determinants of a wide variety of phenomena such as nonepidemic diseases and disorders, accidents, different forms of deviant behavior, and even health.[12] This change represents an expansion in the concept of what might constitute an epidemic and a realization that epidemiologic perspectives need not be restricted to the interpretation of epidemic patterns.[13]

Any epidemiological study, including that of child maltreatment, involves both descriptive and analytic aspects. Descriptive epidemiology concerns the estimation of rates of prevalence and incidence, and of the distributions of these rates according to population characteristics. The objective in analytical epidemiology is to derive and ascertain causal inferences about determinants of child maltreatment. Such inferences form the basis for defining the populations at risk, helping to develop preventive measures, and focusing their application.

Advancement in epidemiologic knowledge requires the presence of a number of elements: clear definitions, classifications useful to both conceptual and applied purposes; specific and objective criteria and empirical indicators; thorough case identification and the absence of systematic bias in unidentified cases; and plausible and verifiable conceptual frameworks or theories that specify explanatory factors and help guide the collection and analysis of data. A realistic assessment of the current status of the epidemiology of child maltreatment would reveal that developments in all of these five elements remain primitive.

Descriptive Aspects

From a descriptive viewpoint, reported cases of abuse and neglect constitute the most meaningful source of data. Estimates of the magnitude of the problem, presented in the foregoing section of this chapter, were based upon the frequency of new reports and thus represent neither the incidence nor the prevalence of child maltreatment. The incidence of maltreatment requires knowledge of the time of onset; such information would be difficult to verify. Furthermore, estimates of the prevalence rates of maltreatment would have required the inclusion of cases already part of the caseloads of agencies. Consequently, considering the present status of definitions, classification, and case identification, the incidence of new reports constitutes an important estimator of the magnitude of the problem.

Inconsistencies among the sampling jurisdictions in the agencies' systems of classification hampered the collection of meaningful data on the characteristics of abused and neglected children, on the characteristics of the alleged abusers, and on the nature of maltreatment. Reports of suspected abuse and neglect in Florida during the year covered in the survey were converted into rates specific to age, sex, and ethnic categories. The significance of these rates (Table 3.2) derives from the fact that they represent the situation in a large state with a diversified population and a nationally acclaimed system for case identification and reporting.

For the heuristic value this might serve, the social distributions of

TABLE 3.2
REPORTED INCIDENCE RATES IN FLORIDA
BY AGE, SEX, AND RACE, WITH
POPULATION-WIDE PROJECTIONS

Characteristics	Reporting Incidence per 1,000 Children*	Numbers in the U.S. Population †
Age Categories		
Under 4	20.9	282,747
4–5	17.2	127,286
6–8	14.7	176,693
9–12	12.2	204,846
13–15	11.7	142,893
16–17	8.5	65,955
Totals	14.2	1,000,420
Sex and Race		
White male	15.2	425,573
White female	16.0	429,166
Black male	13.3	64,168
Black female	14.1	67,689
American Indian male	6.5	1,103
American Indian female	2.7	463
Oriental male	8.8	2,051
Oriental female	9.4	2,193
Spanish-American male	1.1	2,223
Spanish-American female	1.2	2,454
Other male	19.6	1,482
Other female	23.8	1,760
Totals	14.2	1,000,325

*Based on projected 1972 Florida population and 1972 reporting rate.
† Based on 1970 Census.

abuse and neglect indicated by these rates were projected to the national population. As the distributions in Table 3.2 show, the rate of reported maltreatment was highest among children under 4 (20.9 per 1,000), and it declined with advancing age. Grouping children in the age categories presented in the table did not obscure major fluctuations from year to year. To illustrate, the rates for children under the age of 1 and for children aged 1, 2, and 3 did not vary greatly. The same can be said for differences by individual years within each category. Aside from the ethnic category "other," figures in this table also show that the rates of reported abuse and neglect in Florida were highest among whites and lowest among Spanish-Americans. The rates were consistently higher among females than among males across all ethnic groups, except among American Indians, where differences in rates are clearly in the reverse direction.

Continuing with projections based upon the incidence of reporting maltreatment in Florida, Table 3.3 shows the distribution of alleged abusers in the state and the corresponding numbers in the nation for each of the three national estimates presented earlier. We shall designate the estimates based on all sampling jurisdictions, on the state of Florida, and on the high-reporting jurisdictions in the sample as low, medium, and high, respectively. The figures indicate that allegations in reported cases would place mothers as the most frequent abusers, followed by both parents, and then fathers. A sizable proportion of

TABLE 3.3
DISTRIBUTIONS FOR ALLEGED ABUSERS
IN FLORIDA, WITH POPULATION-WIDE PROJECTIONS

	Florida Distribution (percentages)	Projections to U.S. Population *		
Alleged Abusers		Low Estimates	Medium Estimates	High Estimates
Mother	50.5	308,814	505,070	754,999
Father	15.5	94,817	155,075	231,812
Both parents	22.6	138,590	226,666	338,830
Aunt	0.6	3,751	6,136	9,171
Uncle	0.3	1,939	3,171	4,740
Grandfather	0.3	1,686	2,757	4,122
Grandmother	1.2	7,671	12,546	18,755
Grandparents	0.4	2,339	3,826	5,719
Stepmother	0.6	3,562	5,825	8,708
Stepfather	3.4	20,927	34,227	51,165
Foster mother	0.2	1,370	2,241	3,349
Foster father	0.1	443	724	1,082
Babysitter	0.6	3,541	5,790	8,656
Mother's boyfriend	1.4	8,304	13,581	20,301
Neighbor	0.2	1,075	1,759	2,628
Other	1.8	10,769	17,614	26,329
Unknown	0.3	2,086	3,412	5,101
Totals	100.0	611,684	1,000,420	1,495,467

* Based on 1970 Census.

suspected abuse and neglect was attributed to stepparents and mothers' boyfriends. Furthermore, when one considers the relatively smaller proportion of children in foster homes, the significant involvement of foster parents in the maltreatment of children in their custody becomes apparent.

The Florida data also included a classification of the types of abuse and neglect reported. Again, in Table 3.4, the distributions of these types were projected to the same three national estimates of the magnitude of the problem. As would be expected, categories indicative of neglect account for the great majority of cases. Among these categories, children who suffered medical neglect, disorganized family life, abandonment, being left unattended, and the lack of necessities (food, clothing, and/or shelter) exceeded two-thirds of all cases. Among categories suggestive of abuse, beatings, bruises, and sexual molestation constituted the highest proportions, in that order.

Especially significant are projections of the numbers of children who died because of suspected abuse; they ranged from a high of 927 to a low of 380. (Included in this figure are cases of "injury leading to death.") Of all dimensions of child maltreatment, cases resulting in death can be most expected to exhibit the iceberg phenomenon, where the submerged portions are much larger than the visible surfaces. In fact, many deaths in early infancy that were previously attributed to a variety of natural causes are now being seriously considered as, possibly, originating in consciously or subconsciously motivated acts of negligence by parents and guardians.

Analytic Aspects

Advancements in the analytic and the descriptive aspects of epidemiology are highly interdependent and reciprocal in their relations. Clearer concepts and improved estimates of rates and distributions, for example, are mainly helpful in testing explanations and theories; but the resulting increase in the sophistication of the explanations also contributes greatly to the clarification of concepts and classifications.

A plethora of hypotheses has been advanced in attempts to explain child abuse and neglect. Such hypotheses have been related to poverty and economic stress, especially in cases of neglect;[14] to male unemployment, because of the role problems it creates and the economic stress it precipitates;[15] to the culturally sanctioned use of physical force in child rearing;[16] and to other cultural values associated with child care.[17] Child maltreatment has been also explained in terms of the psychopathology of parents, their addictive or alcoholic behavior and their isolation and loneliness, as well as in terms of unwanted pregnancies, the pressure of large numbers of children, and the stress of marital problems.[18] Furthermore, repeated references have been made to child abuse as a learned behavior, in the sense that abusive persons were themselves the victims of abuse during childhood, and that they tend to use their parents' methods with their own children.[19]

In pursuit of additional epidemiological leads, and to assess exist-

TABLE 3.4
DISTRIBUTIONS FOR TYPES OF ABUSE AND NEGLECT
IN FLORIDA, WITH POPULATION-WIDE PROJECTIONS

Type of Abuse and Neglect Suffered	Florida Distributions (percentages)	Projections to the U.S. Population*		
		Low Estimates	Medium Estimates	High Estimates
Death	0.3	211	345	515
Injury leading to death	0.3	169	276	412
Sexual abuse	2.7	16,860	27,575	41,220
Skull fracture	0.1	653	1,068	1,597
Broken bones	0.4	2,402	3,930	5,874
Cuts	0.6	3,836	6,274	9,378
Burns	0.7	4,489	7,342	10,975
Bruises	4.6	28,472	46,568	69,610
Beatings	16.0	97,978	160,245	239,541
Malnutrition	0.8	5,374	8,791	13,139
Medical neglect	16.0	36,650	59,940	89,602
Disorganized family life	31.0	189,655	310,183	463,675
Being abandoned	3.5	21,792	35,640	53,277
Being left unattended	21.6	132,246	216,290	323,321
Lack of food, clothing, shelter	7.5	45,754	74,831	111,861
School problems	2.3	14,479	23,680	35,398
Other	1.5	9,652	15,787	23,599
Unknown	0.1	1,012	1,655	2,473
Totals	100.0	611,684	1,000,420	1,495,467

*Based on 1970 Census.

ing propositions against the experience of respondents in this survey, respondents were asked to characterize those parents and guardians "most likely to *abuse*" and those "most likely to *neglect*" their children. The weighted responses are presented in Tables 3.5 and 3.6. Although many of the responses coincide with propositions in the literature, it would be difficult to ascertain whether these consistencies represent confirmation through truly independent observations or merely reflect the respondents' knowledge of the literature. A comparison of distributions in the two tables clearly indicates that eco-

TABLE 3.5
CHARACTERISTICS OF PERSONS LIKELY
TO ABUSE CHILDREN

Characteristics	Organizations and Responses						
	CPS	PHN	SCH	HMD	HSS	CRT	POL
Had unhappy childhood	71.4	51.0	37.8	35.5	45.2	28.0	25.8
Have unwanted children	5.6	15.8	9.4	9.0	9.3	8.1	9.2
Suffering marital problems	14.9	16.9	8.3	11.7	16.6	14.8	13.3
Are one-parent family	13.1	8.8	8.3	10.6	7.3	5.2	16.8
Are stepparents	1.6	2.0	7.1	5.3	1.9	11.2	13.3
Under emotional pressure	52.4	44.8	35.9	30.5	42.7	29.1	23.8
On low economic level	13.7	14.2	15.0	17.7	12.3	18.7	25.1
Under financial stress	12.6	12.5	20.1	12.1	17.9	14.0	10.3
On high economic level	0.1	2.6	4.3	1.4	2.6	0.5	1.8
Enforcing strict discipline	10.4	3.7	4.2	3.4	8.1	6.6	1.2
Lacking interest in their children	0.0	1.7	2.7	0.4	0.3	3.9	2.6
Lacking education or intelligence	27.3	27.2	24.0	34.5	27.7	29.1	27.9
Selfish	6.7	2.7	12.0	2.6	2.6	3.6	6.8
Have low self-esteem	7.8	3.3	8.9	4.8	7.2	2.9	1.1
Have no friends, family for support	18.3	6.3	3.2	5.7	5.9	2.1	5.4
Hysterical, impulsive	8.5	3.6	6.3	2.3	3.2	3.7	1.3
Have violent life-style	0.0	5.7	1.4	1.9	1.2	0.5	2.5
Young, immature	27.2	29.3	11.7	23.6	22.7	13.7	21.2
Violent, quick-tempered, mean	3.2	4.8	10.2	10.4	9.8	9.4	4.8
Mentally ill and emotionally disturbed	42.9	50.1	48.1	48.1	53.8	46.8	41.1
Physically ill	1.2	7.8	5.3	2.3	5.0	0.1	1.8
Addicted to alcohol, drugs	26.6	18.1	24.7	27.2	17.2	26.0	40.0
Have problem children	5.3	4.9	2.1	7.5	5.2	0.8	2.1
All types—nothing specific	4.8	0.8	2.8	6.9	4.4	12.9	4.0
Other	10.0	13.0	14.2	9.9	10.6	13.3	14.0
Don't know	0.0	1.6	0.8	1.6	2.5	2.6	1.1

NOTE: Column totals may exceed 100 percent because of multiple responses.

TABLE 3.6
CHARACTERISTICS OF PERSONS
LIKELY TO NEGLECT CHILDREN

Characteristics	Organizations and Responses						
	CPS	PHN	SCH	HMD	HSS	CRT	POL
Had unhappy childhood	33.6	31.3	13.0	17.8	23.8	17.0	16.4
Have unwanted children	5.2	15.9	7.0	13.6	13.6	6.8	7.6
Suffering marital problems	5.5	11.7	6.2	7.2	6.7	11.8	8.5
Are one-parent family	11.2	12.5	14.1	12.6	7.6	12.3	24.0
Are stepparents	0.3	1.7	3.0	4.9	0.8	6.1	11.6
Under emotional pressure	27.3	22.6	26.9	19.2	24.0	19.3	15.1
On low economic level	38.1	25.6	33.9	39.7	27.6	30.5	35.6
Under financial stress	15.1	12.6	22.9	13.1	14.2	15.5	10.4
On high economic level	4.9	11.7	15.1	10.3	16.4	12.2	10.1
Enforcing strict discipline	3.3	2.0	2.0	1.9	3.0	1.3	0.6
Lacking interest in their children	0.8	4.2	2.2	5.4	4.8	6.1	4.2
Lacking education or intelligence	40.6	52.3	36.1	47.8	43.5	40.2	27.3
Selfish	13.0	12.2	21.0	9.9	8.3	12.6	13.1
Have low self-esteem	2.9	2.2	3.9	2.4	3.0	2.6	1.2
Have no friends, family for support	7.7	4.3	0.7	4.3	3.6	2.3	0.4
Hysterical, impulsive	2.5	3.1	0.8	1.8	1.0	0.4	0.3
Have violent life-style	0.0	0.6	0.7	0.2	0.9	1.6	0.2
Young, immature	28.2	27.5	13.5	20.3	23.9	11.1	16.1
Violent, quick-tempered, mean	1.4	3.5	2.3	2.4	3.6	2.5	2.1
Mentally ill and emotionally disturbed	42.1	29.4	32.2	32.9	35.1	35.6	25.4
Physically ill	6.0	4.8	5.1	3.2	5.6	2.9	1.6
Addicted to alcohol, drugs	19.5	17.6	20.7	20.1	14.1	29.3	42.4
Have problem children	0.3	4.0	0.4	6.1	3.0	0.8	2.8
All types—nothing specific	2.8	2.5	5.5	8.9	3.3	11.7	3.5
Other	9.6	15.9	22.3	18.0	11.8	9.0	16.5
Don't know	2.0	1.6	2.9	2.0	1.9	1.0	1.3

NOTE: Column totals may exceed 100 percent because of multiple responses.

nomic factors were assigned a greater role in neglect than in abuse. Comparisons across groups of respondents also reveal some interesting differences; social service caseworkers and nurses, for example, tended to mention people suffering emotional pressure more frequently than respondents from police departments and the courts. Alcoholics, drug addicts, mentally ill and emotionally disturbed people, and stepparents were more often mentioned by respondents from law-enforcement agencies.

Aside from the standard sociodemographic identifications, much of the writing and most empirical studies are concerned with the attributes of perpetrators of abuse and neglect, rather than with the characteristics of the children involved. Questions were included in this survey seeking information about the traits of those children more likely, as well as those less likely, to be abused or neglected. Consistently, both abuse and neglect were reported by the various groups of respondents to have occurred less frequently among adopted children than among others. On the other hand, the consensus of respondents was that the mentally retarded and the emotionally disturbed were more likely to be the target of abuse and neglect. These latter observations raise the question of causal direction, that is, whether such forms of maltreatment occur more often among children with these impairments, or whether the impairments are the result of the maltreatment. It is highly probable that there are mutual influences in the relationship. Also included by some respondents as characteristics of children more likely to have been maltreated were "hyperactive," "exceptionally bright," and "young." The latter responses are consistent with the age-specific rates of cases reported in Florida.

Toward an Epidemiological Theory
of Child Maltreatment

It was not the intention of this work to develop an epidemiological theory of child maltreatment, nor are the elements of this kind of theory sufficiently identified, let alone tested in this study. Nevertheless, certain features of such a theory might be anticipated here. First, it must be recognized that child maltreatment is a multicausal phenomenon; the various hypotheses and explanations offered do not necessarily compete with one another. Rather, attempts should be made to integrate hypotheses into cumulative systems which, as they grow, would explain more of the variance in the type of behavior under consideration.

Second, it is important to emphasize that explanations of child maltreatment (or of any other phenomenon for that matter) can be formulated at varying levels of abstraction. Although highly abstract formulations exhibit greater elegance and provide for more economy of thought, they are generally less amenable to verification and are less likely to include guides for action. It is one thing, for example, to relate child maltreatment to feelings of alienation and powerlessness over the forces that shape one's life. To explain maltreatment in terms of unwanted pregnancies or drug addiction constitutes a different and a more concrete level of explanation. Theoretical developments at one level of abstraction do facilitate those at other levels, and, given the current state of epidemiological knowledge, systematic developments at any level on the continuum of abstractness-concreteness should be welcomed.

Third, it is necessary to note that there can be economic, psychological, political, sociological, and other theories of maltreatment, each providing only a partial explanation of the problem. This is an extension of what was mentioned earlier concerning the segmental nature of the explanations provided by any single hypothesis. The same can be said for any given discipline, as well as its basic theories. For example, propositions derived from learning theories can only account for some of the variance in child maltreatment, as can propositions derived from a theory of motivation. It is one thing to use a behavioral pattern such as child maltreatment as an instance for testing a theory of socialization, learning, or the labor market, the interest primarily being to attend and add confirmation to that theory. It is a different matter when the task is to look for explanatory propositions that account for as much variance in child maltreatment as possible, regardless of the theoretical or disciplinary origins of the explanations.

An examination of Abraham Kaplan's two types of theories can illuminate the point under discussion. Building upon distinctions made by Einstein concerning forms of theory construction, Kaplan differentiates between "hierarchical" and "concatenated" theories. A hierarchical theory is organized like "a deductive pyramid in which we rise to fewer and more general laws as we move from conclusions to premises which entail them."[20] In contrast, the concatenated or "pattern" type is one "whose component laws . . . typically . . . converge on some central point, each specifying one of the factors which plays a part in the phenomenon which the theory is to explain."[21]

The hierarchical model is better suited for codifying the principles of the disciplines, that is, their basic and often abstract theory. The concatenated or pattern form, however, is more appropriate for theories explaining given problems, such as child maltreatment, which become the focal point for the convergence of contributing factors. The eclecticism implied in this latter type of theory need not lead to the unsystematic selection of causal factors, nor should the product constitute an unintegrated inventory or collection of these factors. The chief merit of the concatenated form is that it organizes knowledge to offer as complete an explanation of the problem as possible. Furthermore, it allows for the integration of propositions from potentially diverse perspectives, and it can be formulated at concrete enough levels to provide guides for action.

From a substantive viewpoint, child maltreatment is the result of interaction among several constellations of factors. An uninclusive set of categories for such factors would include the perpetrators, the victims, the personal attributes each brings to the interaction, the environmental and situational factors that influence the behavior of both parents and children, and the critical incidents that may act as catalysts triggering episodes of maltreatment. Clear and useful classifications and typologies are sorely needed, for specific types may require differing explanations. The episodic physical violence of a mother against an infant during the early months of life may have little in common with malnutrition because of lack of resources, and both can be expected to vary widely from the sexual abuse of a teenage girl by a parent or guardian.

At present, the difficulties facing the creation of an epidemiological theory of child maltreatment are numerous; to begin with, arguments still rage over such basic etiological questions as whether maltreatment is psychogenic or sociogenic.[22] Useful as they are, each of the propositions in the literature can only offer a segmental explanation of child maltreatment. Lacking at the present time are coherent theoretical frameworks capable of interrelating these propositions. As a result, a number of fruitless tendencies and limitations exist in current analytical material on the problem. Thus hypotheses tend to be offered as mutually exclusive alternatives, rather than as complementary aspects of broader explanatory systems. Furthermore, in the absence of developed theories to guide the identification of significant propositions, the selection of explanatory factors has proceeded on a highly empirical and accidental basis. Thus, the more common explanations are of the *ex post facto* type.

Recognition must be given, however, to efforts toward broader frameworks that attempt to integrate existing classifications and propositions. An example of these is one offered by R. J. Gelles (Figure 3.4) as a social-psychological perspective.[23] Appropriately, the author qualifies the scheme by concluding that "the purpose of presenting this model of factors influencing child abuse is not to suggest an exhaustive list of approaches nor to select one that is superior to the others . . . the purpose is to illustrate the complexity and the interrelationships of the factors that lead to child abuse."[24]

Also useful in presenting a more dynamic, process-oriented picture of the problem of maltreatment is the stress curve. Suggested by Earl Loman Koos and further illustrated by Reuben Hill and others, it has been employed in studies of families during the Depression and under conditions of war separation.[25] The conceptual structure underlying this curve should also assist in organizing the variables involved beyond simple inventories. As shown in Figure 3.5, the wavy line between (a) and (b) represents fluctuations in family relations that remain within the limits of acceptable behavior. At (b) a critical incident may occur that precipitates a crisis situation leading to an incidence of abuse. Severe or repeated incidence might result in a serious problem for the child and most likely for the family as well. Reports and investigations may occur, plunging the family into the level of disorganization indicated by (c). The objective of intervention is to stop the deteriorating conditions and redirect the trend toward greater family adjustment and higher levels of performance, as depicted by (d_1), (d_2), and (d_3). Differences between (a) and (d_1), (d_2), and (d_3) represent the residual problems of the family.

Hypotheses have been formulated concerning the relations between the "angle of recovery" and the levels of performance regained. It is generally postulated that the narrower the angle—that is, the shorter the time needed for recovery of normal functioning—the higher the level of functioning that families attain. It has also been hypothesized that the level of precrisis organization the family had attained is an important factor in determining the level of function re-

FIGURE 3.4

GELLES SOCIAL-PSYCHOLOGICAL MODEL OF CAUSES OF CHILD ABUSE

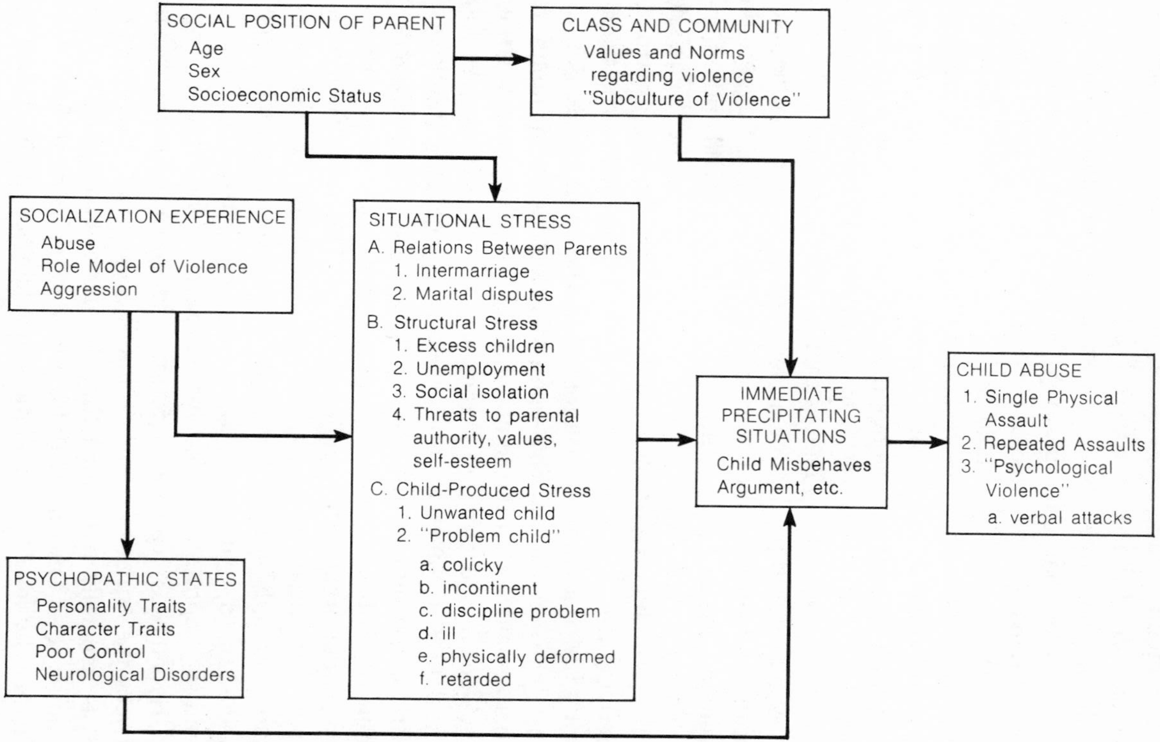

FIGURE 3.5

STRESS CURVE AND FAMILY PERFORMANCE

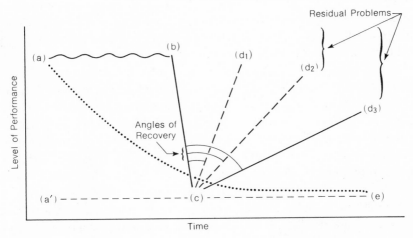

gained after the crisis. It should be mentioned also that the fluctuations between (a) and (b) may include repeated incidents of abuse that do not precipitate major crises. Finally, in terms of severity, of stress, timing, angle of recovery, and the level of functioning regained, the process will vary depending on the perspective from which it is viewed. Considered from the perspectives of the victimized children, the perpetrators, and the family as a whole, different stress curves can be expected to emerge.

Not all cases of child maltreatment follow a pattern in which the points of onset, the points of control of crises, and the angles of recovery can be identified. Certain cases may be best represented by a steady, slow, progressive decline—a pattern of neglect or insidious nonmanifest abuse as indicated by the dotted line (a) to (e) in Figure 3.5. Another type of maltreatment, neglect, often stemming from poverty, is that shown graphically by the broken line (a′) to (e) in the same figure.

The interaction of perpetrators and victims is governed by certain values and norms that constitute the institution of the family. Although child abuse and neglect predate the emergence of the nuclear family typical in modern industrial states, it is still possible that changes in the family have led to an increase in the incidence of abuse and neglect. Fundamental issues need to be explored in this connection. To begin with, we must inquire whether there has been an actual increase in incidence and prevalence, or whether child maltreatment is simply taking different forms and is only becoming more evident through better identification and reporting.

Is the emotional strain of interaction within nuclear families becoming too intense for some parents and children to bear without breaks or other kinds of relief? Did the time children spent with relatives or others in extended families and traditional communities, which often acted as an extension of familial relations, formerly provide such relief? Are families finding it difficult to insulate children from influences conflicting with their traditional values and beliefs, with the result that their controls are challenged beyond tolerance? Are children actually confronted with "generation gaps" that create or accentuate conflicts? Are the emergence and prevalence of contractual forms of social and economic security through public and private programs diminishing the importance of children as providers for the security of the parents in times of need? Are the rise of careerism, notions of self-fulfillment, and similar developments—as well as changes in other institutions, such as the economy, religion, education, and the law—affecting the norms defining parental responsibilities and their dispositions toward fulfillment? To be applicable, a theory addressed to these issues must not only identify those factors in the family that relate to child maltreatment, but also seek to explain their etiologies.

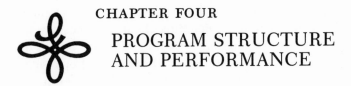

CHAPTER FOUR

PROGRAM STRUCTURE AND PERFORMANCE

ONE OF THE primary objectives of this work was to examine important features of the structure and performance of programs concerned with child abuse and neglect. The presentation of findings related to such an inquiry could be organized in several ways, three of which seemed most promising: around each of the agencies included in the survey; around categories common to much of the current literature on evaluation, such as objectives, structure, input, process, and outcome; or around what might be called functional categories—categories that organize elements of structure and performance in terms of certain problem- and program-oriented topics.

After careful consideration, the third alternative was chosen. The main advantage of functional categories is that they reveal more fully than do the other two alternatives both the interaction among agencies and the dynamics of problems and programs. Furthermore, organizing the discussion and findings around functional topics still permits the roles of the various types of agencies to be discerned, as those roles are reflected in their actions and approaches to problems. The selection of topics followed the sequence of activities in programs addressed to child maltreatment: identification and reporting, response to reporting, availability and provision of services, legal intervention and the problems of custody and placement, decision-making, and the coordination of programs.

IDENTIFICATION AND REPORTING

The importance of accuracy and proper timing in identifying and reporting child maltreatment cannot be overstated. Case finding is most important, as the first step to providing protective and treatment services. Furthermore, knowledge of the social distributions of abuse and neglect, and of the factors precipitating them, is necessary for identifying populations at risk and for mounting effective efforts toward prevention. And, as mentioned earlier, the quality of epidemiological knowledge concerning these problems depends largely upon the validity of available incidence data. In the following paragraphs, we will explore the sources, procedures, and limitations involved in identifying and reporting child maltreatment, as they apply to the various agencies.

The investigative role and the authority of child protection agencies, the police, and the courts have made them the most frequent recipients of reports. Schools and hospitals also constitute important settings for the observation of children; for, although they may receive reports from outside sources about suspected abuse and neglect, personnel in these two types of institutions have greater opportunity to identify cases on their own. Finally, cases may come to the attention of public health nurses from a variety of sources, as well as from their own observations during home visits.

Respondents from child protective agencies, police and sheriff's departments, and public health nursing agencies were asked identical questions concerning the sources from which they learned about suspected abuse and neglect during the year prior to the survey. Essentially the same information was sought from respondents in the courts, who were asked about the origins of affidavits filed in connection with these problems. Data obtained from these agencies are presented in Table 4.1. Sources varied markedly from one receiving agency to another. Relatives, friends, and neighbors were responsible for large proportions of reports to the police (48.6 percent) and to child protective services (31.1 percent). These latter agencies seem to have been involved in a relatively high rate of referrals to public health nurses (21.9 percent), as were hospitals and clinics (18.4 percent). Schools, hospitals and clinics, other social welfare services, and the police and sheriff's departments all contributed in similar levels to reports reaching child protective agencies. It is important to note the relatively low exchange between these agencies and the police in terms of the levels of reciprocal reporting or referral. By far the greatest proportion of affidavits submitted to the courts emanated from protective agencies. Responses in the table confirm the disinclination on the part of persons in private practice, including physicians, to become involved in reporting child maltreatment to public agencies. Finally, it should be added that, of all the cases that became known to them, public health nurses themselves "came across" 44.9 percent during home visits, 17 percent in schools, and 38.1 percent in settings such as clinics, child health conferences, and others.

Although varying somewhat in classification, the distribution of sources of reports in the state of Florida for the year comparable to that covered in the survey shows similar trends. Family and relatives were responsible for 24 percent of the reports and neighbors for 24.8 percent. Schools were the source of reports in only 6.5 percent of the

TABLE 4.1
SOURCES OF REPORTS, REFERRALS, AND AFFIDAVITS TO
AGENCIES IN SURVEY SAMPLE

Sources	Receiving Agencies			
	CPS	PHN	CRT	POL
Public health departments	3.6	. . . .	1.3	1.8
Prosecuting attorney's offices	2.5	1.4	14.8	2.2
Courts	7.0	0.8	. . . .	1.7
Hospitals and clinics	11.9	18.4	1.4	9.3
Child protective agencies	. . . .	21.9	43.0	8.7
Other social welfare services	12.2	5.4	13.6	3.5
Schools	12.1	13.5	1.8	10.5
Police and sheriff's departments	11.0	0.9	8.7	. . . .
Private and voluntary agencies	2.3	1.5	0.9	0.9
Other agencies	1.2	11.9	3.9	6.0
Clergymen	0.5	0.2	0.0	0.5
Private physicians	2.4	5.1	0.5	3.1
Private psychologists	0.3	0.0	0.0	0.1
Other professionals	0.3	1.3	0.2	0.4
Relatives	15.1	8.2	7.8	21.5
Friends and neighbors	16.0	9.2	1.6	27.1
Other laymen	1.7	0.2	0.5	2.6

cases and day-care centers in 0.4 percent. Neither hospitals nor private physicians were a major source of reports in Florida; they accounted for 1.3 percent and 1.4 percent of the cases, respectively.

In interviews with hospital medical and social services personnel, attempts were made to distinguish between cases identified within the hospitals by their own staff and those referred by other agencies or individuals. The average estimates given by the medical personnel for these two sources of identification were 83.2 percent and 16.8 percent, respectively. The corresponding estimates given by social services departments in the same hospitals were 85.0 percent and 15.0 percent.

Clearly, the overwhelming majority of cases of abuse and neglect that became known to hospitals were identified by their own personnel. When asked who brought or referred to the hospitals children who were subsequently suspected as victims of maltreatment, the two groups of respondents gave consistent replies. Respondents from social services placed parents first (61.4 percent), other relatives and neighbors second (13.8 percent), and private physicians third (10.9 percent), with other hospitals accounting for about 1.1 percent of the referrals.

Answers from social service and medical department personnel concerning referral sources for cases already suspected of abuse and neglect were also fairly consistent. According to responses from social service personnel, child protective agencies accounted for 32.2 percent of such referrals, the police for 25.3 percent, physicians in private practice for 17.4 percent, and other hospitals for 6.7 percent. Private physicians seem to refer more cases to hospitals than to other public agencies, probably because they are primarily concerned with medical and health care. Unstructured interviews with physicians also revealed that many in private practice refer suspected cases of child maltreatment to hospitals as a way of transferring to those institutions the responsibility for reporting such cases. Once again, this illustrates the influence of role conflict, discussed in chapter 3.

Because of the nature of school systems, information different from that requested of other agencies was sought from them. In 33.3 percent of the cases identified during the year covered in the survey, school personnel were alerted by the abused or neglected children themselves. Siblings were the source of information in 2.4 percent of the cases and other pupils in 8.3 percent. In 56 percent of the cases, persons outside the school systems or other agencies brought incidents to the attention of the school. The most frequently mentioned were informal sources such as relatives, friends and neighbors of the families involved, parents of the victims, and anonymous callers. It appears that schools are not well connected with the other parts of the organizational network concerned with this problem, at least in regard to being informed about cases that become known to other

TABLE 4.2

ABUSE AND NEGLECT DISTRIBUTIONS AMONG CHILDREN
KNOWN TO AGENCIES IN SURVEY SAMPLE

	Cases Known to Agencies	
Agencies and Programs	*Abuse*	*Neglect*
	(percentages)	
Child protective services	27.0	73.0
Public health nursing services	30.8	69.2
Schools	50.4	49.6
Hospital medical departments	63.4	36.6
Hospital social services	60.2	39.8
Courts	25.4	74.6
Police and sheriff's departments	46.6	53.4

agencies. We further inquired about the proportions of cases first reported by persons occupying various positions in the schools. The average weighted responses show that 50.8 percent were first reported by teachers, 9.4 percent by counselors, 10.6 percent by school nurses, 0.1 percent by school physicians, 5.8 percent by school social workers, 7.5 percent by principals and other administrators, and 15.8 percent by others.

Finally, it should be of interest to note variations in the relative proportions of abuse and of neglect among cases reported or referred to the agencies included in the survey. As might be expected, the distribution in Table 4.2 shows a greater proportion of child abuse among cases that came to the attention of hospitals. The ratios of abuse to neglect were also greater for the schools and the police than for child protective and public health nursing services. The ratios for affidavits submitted to the courts were similar to those reported by protective agencies. Because of the lack of criteria for clearly differentiating abuse and neglect (many jurisdictions make no distinction at all), these ratios should be interpreted with caution.

The processes of identifying and reporting child maltreatment may constitute a single step, such as a call from an observer to an agency, or they may entail multiple steps within and across agencies. Procedures governing these processes, if any, are particularly important in agencies where relatively sizable proportions of the cases are identified internally, through the agency and its staff, rather than reported from outside sources. Identification and reporting in schools, hospitals, and public health nursing agencies entail such processes. Respondents from these three agencies were asked about the existence "of specific procedures for reporting suspected cases of abuse and neglect." This inquiry was followed by questions as to whether these procedures were set forth in written form, how regularly they were followed, and the locus of decisions about reporting on behalf of the agency.

Table 4.3 presents some of this information. School systems and public health nursing agencies representing about half the U.S. population had written instructions on procedures for reporting suspected cases of child maltreatment. Hospital medical and social services personnel, however, differed in their responses to these questions. According to the medical personnel, hospitals most accessible to only 46 percent of the population had written instructions for reporting child maltreatment; the corresponding figure for respondents from hospital social services departments was 60.2 percent. The reason for the variation might be the social service personnel's increased awareness of the existence of reporting procedures; in some hospitals, moreover, such rules are specific to these departments. Most likely a combination of these and other factors contributed to the discrepancies. To be noted are the proportions of the population represented by agencies for which no written instructions and no set procedures for reporting existed; this ranged from a high of 35.2 percent for hospital medical programs to a low of 21.9 percent for hospital social services.

Even when established, reporting procedures were not always fol-

TABLE 4.3
REPORTING PROCEDURES IN SCHOOL SYSTEMS, HOSPITALS,
AND PUBLIC HEALTH NURSING AGENCIES

Reporting Procedures	Organizations and Responses			
	PHN	SCH	HMD	HSS
Availability of procedures and instructions				
Written instructions available	48.6	50.3	46.0	60.2
Procedures exist	21.4	18.1	16.5	16.5
Unsure of form	0.0	2.6	2.3	1.4
No reporting procedures or instructions	30.0	28.8	35.2	21.9
Where procedure exists, how regularly followed?				
Almost always	87.8	78.8	83.4	84.9
Often	7.3	14.0	8.8	7.1
Sometimes	4.7	4.4	5.7	7.6
Occasionally	0.2	1.6	2.1	0.2
Hardly ever	0.0	1.3	0.0	0.2
Is reporting to other agencies assigned to specific department or person?				
Yes	23.2	54.9	47.1	65.8
No	46.5	16.0	17.0	11.2
No reporting procedures	30.3	29.1	35.9	22.9

lowed (Table 4.3); however, the predominant opinion was that they were used "often" or "almost always." Adherence to such procedures only "sometimes" or "less frequently" ranged from 7.3 percent for school systems to 4.9 percent for public health nursing agencies. Medical and social services personnel in hospitals were very similar in their estimates of low adherence (7.8 percent and 8 percent, respectively). The most frequently mentioned reasons for failure to follow reporting procedures in the various agencies included lack of training in and knowledge of these procedures, doubts about the sufficiency of evidence, and reluctance or fear at the thought of getting involved. Ignorance about procedures was most characteristic of hospital personnel, while fear of getting involved was most common in those from the schools. Formalized written instructions on procedures for reporting were more likely to have been followed than unwritten ones. Hospitals and schools seemed to centralize procedures for reporting to other agencies in the hands of one person or one department more frequently than did public health nursing organizations (Table 4.3). These responsibilities were most often undertaken by heads of departments, supervisors, principals, or assistant principals, although school counselors were also frequently mentioned.

Some measure of current limitations in reporting and of the magnitude of the problem might be inferred from comparisons among the three estimates given earlier and their projections to the national population. To probe further into other aspects of these limitations, questions were asked about the consistency with which the various sources reported suspected abuse and neglect cases to agencies. When addressed to child protective agencies, police and sheriff's departments, and public health nursing agencies, inquiries covered a broad range of sources. Assessments given by interviewees from these three agencies are presented in Tables 4.4, 4.5, and 4.6. A five-point scale was used to record responses ranging from "almost always" to "hardly ever." Since protection agencies and the police are the legally mandated or most common recipients of reports, responses given by their personnel are of particular significance. If we consider the latter three responses ("sometimes," "occasionally," and "hardly ever") to represent deficiencies in reporting suspected cases, the distributions in these three tables cast serious doubt on the adequacy of current levels of identification and reporting.

The reasons given by personnel from child protective agencies for inadequate reporting by others varied according to the sources of the reports included in Table 4.4. In regard to the police, public health nurses, and other law-enforcement and welfare agencies, the most frequently mentioned reasons were that these agencies handled the problem themselves and that their staff members lacked sufficient knowledge about the role of protective services. The reasons offered most frequently for nonreporting by professionals in independent practice, and especially by physicians, included the desire to maintain confidentiality, reluctance to become involved, fear of loss of patients and clients, and the professionals' belief that they should handle the problem themselves. These professionals' lack of awareness of the child protective agencies and their role also significantly limited the likelihood of their reporting. Underreporting from such informal sources as family members, other relatives, friends, and neighbors

TABLE 4.4
ESTIMATES OF REPORTING TO CHILD PROTECTIVE SERVICES

	Likelihood of Reporting to CPS				
Source of Identification	Almost Always	Often	Some-times	Occa-sionally	Hardly Ever
Public health nursing agencies	40.4	26.6	17.6	8.1	7.2
Hospitals	29.4	33.6	19.6	10.1	7.3
Welfare and social services	53.6	26.3	14.3	3.3	2.4
Schools	26.1	39.8	21.4	11.2	1.6
Police and sheriff's departments	47.0	27.4	18.2	4.2	3.2
Private and voluntary agencies	24.1	16.1	28.4	11.3	20.0
Other agencies	28.5	11.0	19.4	14.0	27.0
Clergymen	9.5	11.9	13.2	22.2	43.2
Physicians	14.5	13.2	20.3	18.7	33.2
Psychologists and counselors	13.3	9.2	9.9	9.7	57.9
Other professionals	14.9	7.1	15.9	16.4	45.7
Relatives and family	9.7	35.5	37.5	15.1	2.2
Friends and neighbors	6.2	40.6	36.7	11.4	5.0
Other laymen	11.6	13.6	32.6	21.4	20.8

TABLE 4.5
ESTIMATES OF REPORTING TO POLICE
AND SHERIFF'S DEPARTMENTS

	Likelihood of Reporting to POL				
Sources of Identification	Almost Always	Often	Some-times	Occa-sionally	Hardly Ever
Public health nursing agencies	38.4	9.1	8.8	7.4	36.3
Hospitals	47.0	13.3	11.4	7.6	20.8
Child protective services	45.4	9.9	11.4	4.7	28.6
Welfare and social services	30.1	14.2	10.4	6.4	38.8
Schools	39.5	12.7	16.1	14.1	17.6
Private and voluntary agencies	19.1	10.0	9.9	7.6	53.4
Other agencies	24.6	9.2	9.0	3.9	53.4
Clergymen	22.6	6.5	7.8	11.3	51.7
Physicians	30.8	9.6	11.4	12.4	35.8
Psychologists and counselors	10.6	3.9	9.8	5.6	70.1
Other professionals	23.9	3.8	4.8	8.0	59.5
Relatives and family	19.3	22.6	31.5	12.7	13.9
Friends and neighbors	16.5	32.1	24.9	14.1	12.4
Other laymen	21.4	15.2	16.6	9.3	37.5

TABLE 4.6
ESTIMATES OF REPORTING TO PUBLIC HEALTH
NURSING AGENCIES

Sources of Identification	Likelihood of Reporting to PHN				
	Almost Always	Often	Some-times	Occa-sionally	Hardly Ever
Hospitals	20.1	11.5	16.0	17.6	34.8
Child protective services	30.4	14.9	13.0	10.6	31.2
Welfare and social services	20.3	10.6	18.1	13.3	37.7
Schools	20.0	21.3	12.6	12.2	34.0
Police and sheriff's departments	11.8	3.6	8.6	12.7	63.2
Private and voluntary agencies	9.8	4.0	9.9	16.0	60.3
Other agencies	22.8	12.2	10.5	4.1	50.5
Clergymen	9.3	7.8	9.3	9.6	63.9
Physicians	11.0	5.1	15.3	18.4	50.2
Psychologists and counselors	7.4	1.6	7.9	4.3	78.8
Other professionals	4.4	3.7	14.3	9.1	68.5
Relatives and family	7.9	17.1	24.7	23.5	26.7
Friends and neighbors	12.4	18.2	21.2	24.0	24.2
Other laymen	8.9	4.8	9.7	13.3	63.3

was attributed primarily to the desire not to get involved, concern for personal ramifications, and the impulse to protect the perpetrators.

Medical and social service respondents from the hospitals were asked to assess the likelihood of physicians and nurses in hospital settings reporting cases of abuse and neglect about which they had definite knowledge (Table 4.7). The evaluations of medical respondents were uniformly more optimistic than those of the social service personnel. According to both, however, nurses were more likely than physicians to have reported cases that came to their attention. It is important to note the much greater probability of reporting by physicians in hospitals (even when considering their lower assessment by social service personnel) compared to physicians in private practice, as assessed by respondents from protective agencies (Table 4.4) from police and sheriff's departments (Table 4.5), and public health nursing agencies (Table 4.6). Nevertheless, the likelihood of reporting by physicians in hospitals was still lower than might have been expected. The reasons given for nonreporting by physicians and nurses in hospital settings centered around insufficiency of evidence, lack of

TABLE 4.7
ESTIMATES BY MEDICAL AND SOCIAL SERVICES RESPONDENTS
OF REPORTING BY HOSPITAL PHYSICIANS AND NURSES

Likelihood of Reporting	Estimate by Medical Personnel		Estimate by Social Services Personnel	
	For Physicians	For Nurses	For Physicians	For Nurses
Almost always	65.8	82.4	55.1	70.2
Often	17.3	9.9	16.0	15.6
Sometimes	12.9	3.4	18.9	9.3
Occasionally	3.0	1.8	6.7	1.6
Hardly ever	1.0	2.6	3.3	3.3

knowledge and experience in handling the problem, and the desire not to get involved because of inconvenience, fear of losing time, or fear of other consequences. Finally, as illustrated in Table 4.8, the hospital departments least likely to report suspected child maltreatment were emergency-room facilities, followed by out-patient services. Conversely, these problems were most likely to have been reported if observed in the in-patient wards. The reasons given for hospital departments' failure to report were similar to those mentioned above for physicians and nurses in hospital settings. In addition, understaffing was cited frequently as a reason for inadequacies of reporting in a number of settings.

Interviews in the school systems included similar questions aimed

TABLE 4.8
ESTIMATES BY MEDICAL AND SOCIAL SERVICES RESPONDENTS
OF UNDERREPORTING IN VARIOUS HOSPITAL DEPARTMENTS

Hospital Operations	Estimates	
	By Hospital Medical Staff	By Social Services Staff
Where Underreporting Most Likely to Occur:		
Emergency rooms	40.6	23.4
Out-patient services	16.8	24.3
In-patient wards	8.9	12.6
No differences	31.8	35.4
Don't know	3.2	6.1

NOTE: Column totals may exceed 100 percent because of multiple responses.

at evaluating the probability of various personnel having reported suspected cases of abuse and neglect. Table 4.9 presents the results of these assessments. Given the level of reporting accorded school systems by other agencies (Tables 4.4, 4.5, and 4.6), respondents' ratings of the likelihood of reporting by school personnel seem rather high. Nevertheless, the distributions in Table 4.9 are revealing in terms of the practices of personnel in various positions. Considering that the two responses "almost always," and "often," represent adequate levels of reporting, the assessments show school social workers as most inclined to report suspected cases and school physicians as the least inclined. In fact, school physicians, more than any other category, were described by respondents as "hardly ever" reporting. The reasons given for nonreporting by school professionals were similar to those mentioned for hospital personnel, physicians, and nurses: inadequate evidence; reluctance to get involved; a concern for potential consequences, a lack of knowledge and experience with reporting on the part of some, especially teachers; and an inclination to handle the problem personally on the part of others, especially social workers, nurses, and counselors.

Personnel from school systems, public health nursing services, and hospital medical departments were asked whether their organizations had "standard screening procedures which may detect child abuse and neglect" among children they see professionally. Interestingly, an affirmative response to this question was much more prevalent for school systems and public health nursing agencies than for hospital medical departments (Table 4.10). Hospitals representing only 13.1 percent of the population had developed standard screening procedures. Although such procedures were more common in schools and in public health nursing, even these two services had only established standard screening procedures for areas covering less than half the U.S. population; furthermore, even when these screening procedures existed, they were not always followed. For a significant proportion of the population, screening procedures were followed only in suspected cases of abuse and neglect, for children being admitted to schools, for pupils in certain grade levels, and for children covered by certain programs, especially Medicaid. In most cases, standard screening in schools consisted of physical examinations, fol-

TABLE 4.9
ESTIMATES OF REPORTING BY SCHOOL PERSONNEL

Personnel Category	Likelihood of Reporting				
	Almost Always	Often	Some-times	Occa-sionally	Hardly Ever
Teachers	64.8	19.3	9.9	3.9	2.1
Counselors	78.4	12.0	4.4	2.7	2.4
Nurses	90.4	3.4	4.5	0.2	1.6
Principals	78.6	10.1	9.0	1.7	0.7
Physicians	76.6	4.0	5.3	3.3	10.8
Social workers	91.2	4.8	2.4	0.2	1.4
Others	78.0	9.0	8.6	2.2	2.2

TABLE 4.10
SCREENING PROCEDURES IN SCHOOL SYSTEMS,
PUBLIC HEALTH NURSING AGENCIES, AND
HOSPITAL MEDICAL DEPARTMENTS

Standard Screening	Organizations and Responses		
	PHN	SCH	HMD
None employed	53.5	56.1	86.5
Screening applied to all children	31.2	31.4	8.3
Screening applied selectively	14.3	11.8	4.8
Don't know	1.0	0.6	0.4

TABLE 4.11
ESTIMATED UNDERREPORTING OF ABUSE AND OF
NEGLECT IN RESPONDENTS' COMMUNITIES

Degree of Underreporting	Organizations and Responses						
	CPS	PHN	SCH	HMD	HSS	CRT	POL
Child Abuse							
A great deal	45.0	40.5	29.8	24.3	34.7	40.9	30.6
Some	40.6	49.0	46.4	34.7	39.1	42.1	49.5
None	14.4	10.5	23.8	41.0	26.1	17.0	19.9
Child Neglect							
A great deal	33.4	50.0	37.7	40.5	50.4	45.1	47.2
Some	35.3	41.2	40.2	33.9	31.4	32.5	36.8
None	31.3	8.8	22.1	25.6	18.3	22.4	15.9

lowed by observations of suspected cases for such manifestations of abuse and neglect as bruises, scars, injuries, or emotional problems. It is doubtful, however, that the routine medical examinations administered for school entrants were specifically oriented toward the identification of these problems.

The great majority of respondents from all agencies and programs felt that child abuse and neglect were being underreported in their communities (Table 4.11). When it came to assessing the degree of underreporting, however, opinions were divided. "A great deal" of underreporting was more characteristic of responses from child protective agencies (45 percent), the courts (40.9 percent), and public health departments (40.5 percent) than from the other groups interviewed. "No underreporting" was claimed most often by hospital medical personnel (41.0 percent) and least often by public health nursing staff (10.5 percent).

With minor exceptions, most respondents who believed abuse and neglect were underreported also felt that selectivity played a role in underreporting, and that it was influenced by the characteristics of both victims and perpetrators. Although both high and low socioeconomic levels were mentioned as categories of parents for whom underreporting is most likely to happen, much larger proportions of the weighted responses mentioned people in the higher socioeconomic levels. To concentrate on the most common recipients of reports, child protective services, the proportions citing parents from high and low socioeconomic levels were 70.9 percent and 15.5 percent, respectively.

Another factor in selectivity was the ages of children. Although all ages were mentioned, the most frequently stated view was that underreporting occurred for children under 5 years of age. Estimates of underreporting decreased as the ages of possible victims increased. Underreporting was also believed to have been characteristic for physically and mentally handicapped children.

Respondents from protective agencies and the police were also asked about selectivity in confirmation rates, as well as the associated characteristics of perpetrators and children. Their weighted responses affirm the existence of selectivity in confirming maltreatment according to such characteristics. The proportion of protective agencies that confirmed the influence of parents' characteristics on cases of abuse was 57.5 percent, and on cases of neglect, 56.7 percent. The corresponding weighted responses concerning the influence of children's attributes were 24.2 percent and 20.6 percent, respectively. Affirmative opinions about selectivity were somewhat fewer among respondents from the police.

"Have there been any special efforts in the last few years in this area or in the state as a whole to get cases of child abuse and neglect identified and reported?" Personnel from all agencies and programs included in the survey had the opportunity to respond to this and to three follow-up questions about the nature of such efforts, their administrative boundaries (state or local), and their effects upon reporting (Table 4.12). Most of the efforts seen have been directed toward legal changes and toward professional and public education. It is important to note differences in the prevalence of negative opinions (those indicating that no efforts had been undertaken) which ranged from a high of 44.6 percent for hospital medical respondents to a low of 0.3 percent for child protective services. Public health nurses, the police, and respondents from child protective agencies were equally distributed in their views as to the scope of efforts, state versus local. The courts were more likely to see the effects as statewide. This is not surprising, since important legal changes usually originate at the state level. More of the weighted responses from schools and hospitals indicated that developments toward enhanced reporting were local rather than statewide. The greatest claims for the effectiveness of such efforts came from child protective agencies (53.1 percent), followed by the police (46.5 percent). Considering the assessments of all respondents, the effects of attempts to enhance reporting seem to be limited.

RESPONSE TO REPORTS

Although police departments have personnel on duty at all hours, only 32.1 percent of the population live in communities where child protection agencies provide such coverage. Also, public health nursing agencies available to only 5.3 percent of the population reported around-the-clock availability for their personnel. In protective agencies serving 50.4 percent of the population and in public health nursing divisions serving 49.5 percent, a caseworker or a nurse "always made a home visit during the same day that a new case of suspected child *abuse* was reported." In all of the other jurisdictions, 55.8 percent of the cases were visited by caseworkers from protective services in the same day and 82.4 percent during the week. The corresponding proportions visited by nurses from public health departments were 57.3 percent and 83 percent respectively. In practically all of the cases considered emergencies, a police officer or a sheriff's deputy went to the home within hours. This was also the case in regard to nonemergency situations for over 85 percent of the population. Most of the departments representing the other 15 percent conducted visits to the homes within the day. Distinctions between

TABLE 4.12
SPECIAL IDENTIFICATION AND REPORTING EFFORTS

Special Efforts	Organizations and Responses						
	CPS	PHN	SCH	HMD	HSS	CRT	POL
Nature of Efforts							
None undertaken	0.3	8.0	33.7	44.6	23.4	17.5	25.9
24-hour telephone	3.0	3.7	0.8	0.0	2.6	1.2	2.6
Broad-based team	13.9	13.9	9.3	6.7	12.0	6.4	7.6
Changed laws	38.5	31.0	17.7	11.2	14.3	42.7	24.1
New reporting system	25.8	22.1	8.4	5.3	10.0	12.2	6.9
Improved CPS service	0.0	2.5	0.0	1.6	0.0	6.5	0.0
Public education	43.3	16.9	4.9	11.9	22.7	22.7	21.9
Professional education	17.7	23.1	29.2	20.2	27.6	11.9	16.7
Interagency cooperation	10.7	11.1	7.1	3.1	9.1	5.0	7.5
Other	1.5	5.4	8.6	4.1	5.1	2.0	11.7
Don't know	1.3	0.6	0.4	3.4	3.6	6.3	3.1
Level of Efforts							
State	48.4	47.9	29.1	30.3	28.0	62.7	50.1
Regional	0.7	1.2	0.0	0.2	1.0	0.0	0.3
Local	50.9	50.9	70.9	69.5	71.0	37.3	49.6
Effects of Efforts on Reporting							
Increased greatly	53.1	38.0	29.1	30.0	32.5	32.6	46.5
Increased somewhat	39.4	44.5	53.6	58.5	48.8	53.8	32.2
Not increased	7.5	17.5	17.2	11.5	18.7	13.6	21.3

NOTE: Column totals may exceed 100 percent because of multiple responses.

emergencies and nonemergencies were based largely on the information given by callers and the degree of threat or danger to life or health the incident was believed to pose.

When home visits were not conducted by child protection agencies and the police for all cases reported to them, respondents from the two agencies were asked about the procedures used to ascertain which calls were likely to have some verifiable basis. A list of the

TABLE 4.13
VALIDATING PROCEDURES FOR REPORTS

Procedures	Organizations and Responses	
	CPS	POL
Eliminating anonymous telephone calls	4.6	3.7
Asking caller for details	10.8	3.6
Determining urgency from caller	8.4	9.1
Eliminating previously unsubstantiated calls	12.3	9.4
Asking caller to report in person	0.0	3.6
Obtaining confirmation from other agency	38.1	39.3
Obtaining confirmation from other people	14.6	3.2
Checking on previous reports	15.4	4.8
Using best judgment	14.9	7.9
Referring caller to probate court	1.0	0.0
Referring caller to other agency	3.3	27.3
Other	6.8	9.9
Screening all neglect calls and visiting all abuse calls	6.2	1.3

NOTE: Column totals may exceed 100 percent because of multiple responses.

responses is presented in Table 4.13, demonstrating that the most common procedure for both agencies was to obtain confirmation from other agencies. Protective agencies also relied on confirmation from other people and from previous reports, while the police were likely to handle the problem through referral cases to other agencies.

Police officers and deputies representing 52.4 percent of the population never had staff members of other agencies accompany them in making the first visit to a home where a child was reported to have been abused or neglected. In the remaining 47.6 percent, officers and deputies were at times accompanied by personnel from other agencies. The most commonly mentioned agencies in this regard were child protection services, other divisions of welfare services, and probation and juvenile officers, respectively. After they had become acquainted with a case, officers and deputies representing 76.2 percent of the population might have asked staff members of other agencies to come to the homes. In this case, child protective services, other welfare services, and public health nursing agencies were the most commonly mentioned. In order of frequency of mention, the reasons given for representatives of these agencies to enter cases included requests that they conduct investigations, that they take over cases, that they arrange for the placement of children, and that they undertake counseling. It is important to point out that 14.5 percent of the population resided in the jurisdictions of police and sheriff's departments whose officers neither called on personnel from other agencies to accompany them during the first visit nor went to homes after these law-enforcement officers had become acquainted with the case.

The average percentages of cases in which the respondents found it necessary to remove children from their homes were as follows:

> 4.6 in almost all of the cases
> 9.1 in more than half of the cases
> 12.6 in about half the cases
> 35.6 in less than half the cases
> 38.1 in almost none of the cases

Respondents from child protective services, public health nursing agencies, and hospital social services were asked about the proportions of the abuse and neglect cases coming to the attention of their agencies that, in their opinions, warranted the children's temporary separation from their families (Table 4.14). Although opinions varied, the figures reveal a strong reluctance, especially on the part of respondents from public health departments, to advise the removal of children. Descriptions of the conditions viewed as warranting temporary removal of children were given in general terms (Table 4.15); considerations included the seriousness of abuse, threats to health and life, and the children's need for protection.

The length of time required for investigations conducted by the police may vary from a few hours to over one month. For 27.7 percent of the population, such investigations were usually completed within one day (24 hours); the usual duration for another 29 percent

TABLE 4.14
CASES WARRANTING TEMPORARY SEPARATION

Estimated Percentages	Organizations and Responses		
	CPS	PHN	HSS
Less than 25	54.0	70.6	47.4
25–49	19.4	9.6	21.2
50–74	20.4	11.4	15.4
75–99	2.6	3.7	8.8
100	3.7	4.7	7.2

did not exceed one week; and the time required for 14.3 percent stretched from more than one week to over one month. Finally, the respondents for 29 percent failed to specify duration because of "variations among cases." The sources most commonly pursued by police officers for evidence of abuse and neglect were witnesses (including neighbors and relatives), photographs, medical reports and physicians' statements, and observation of the children's conditions. Less frequently mentioned were such sources of evidence as the statements of children, parents, or other reporting persons.

TABLE 4.15
CONDITIONS WARRANTING TEMPORARY SEPARATION

Conditions	Organizations and Responses		
	CPS	PHN	HSS
No one to care for child	2.4	1.8	4.3
Parent incapable of care	17.1	8.5	16.4
Parent uncooperative, unresponsive	16.1	7.6	17.7
Parents in treatment	5.2	1.8	5.5
Serious abuse has occurred	24.2	21.0	18.9
Severe threat to child still present	40.0	13.7	10.5
ighting in home	7.5	7.9	9.5
Protection, help needed by child	34.4	33.5	26.1
No food, heat, water, other necessities	5.1	2.7	2.1
Parents request child be taken	. . . .	. . . .	2.6
Emergency situation	0.1	. . . .	0.3
All cases	1.2	. . . .	2.2
Never	1.3	18.9	20.0
Other	8.6	16.0	6.6

NOTE: Column totals may exceed 100 percent because of multiple responses.

Law-enforcement officers, hospital medical personnel, and respondents from school systems were asked about the type of evidence they look for in cases of abuse and of neglect. Their answers (Table 4.16) show a heavy reliance on such physical signs as injuries, bruises, malnutrition, and other indications of improper treatment and care. The relatively more frequent mention of the "home environment" by police officers is not surprising, since they are the most likely to have visited the victims' homes.

As has been illustrated, the initial response to reporting entails many investigatory functions; verifying claims of abuse and neglect,

TABLE 4.16
EVIDENCE SOUGHT BY POLICE, HOSPITAL MEDICAL DEPARTMENTS,
AND SCHOOL SYSTEMS

	Abuse			Neglect		
Types of Evidence	SCH	HMD	POL	SCH	HMD	POL
Signs of physical abuse	88.9	56.4	89.9	79.8	80.0	69.0
Emotional injuries	17.5	11.5	12.0	18.5	30.9	10.1
General condition	5.4	3.0	7.2	8.4	6.5	9.1
Home environment	....	....	18.7	1.7	0.1	66.3
Alcoholism or drug abuse	....	0.2	1.4	0.7	0.9	1.7
Child's own report of incident	37.1	0.8	6.3	17.1	1.0	1.4
Child left alone	....	....	....	2.4	3.4	17.2
Parent's reaction to child	0.5	11.1	7.6	1.0	8.7	4.4
Child absent from school	5.6	....	....	17.3	....	....
Witnesses' observations	4.6	0.5	2.0	6.5	2.4	2.4
Abuse weapons	....	0.7	4.9	....	....	....
Repetition of incidents, reports, injuries	2.7	20.0	....	1.3	5.2	....
Injuries, conditions with implausible explanations	3.5	47.8	....	....	3.8	....
Delay in obtaining medical attention	0.1	1.8	....	0.9	4.7	....
Previous injuries	1.0	12.0	....	....	....	....
Poor health, no apparent cause	1.2	1.7	....	....	7.9	....
Reports, information from other agencies	....	0.3	....	....	0.2	....
Family history or background	0.2	4.9	....	0.3	6.5	....
No money for lunch	0.4	....	....	2.9	....	....
School performance	2.0	....	....	4.7	....	....
Other	1.0	1.0	4.5	3.0	1.1	2.4

NOTE: Column totals may exceed 100 percent because of multiple responses.

assessing the severity of damage and the risks of further maltreatment, and collecting such evidence as might be needed for juvenile,
family, or criminal court proceedings. These initial responses to sus-
picions or reports of child abuse and neglect become the basis for
social welfare services and/or legal intervention.

SERVICES: PROVISION AND AVAILABILITY

The first priority in intervention on behalf of abused and neglected
children should be given to medical attention and health care. Hospital medical personnel were asked what happened to children when
abuse and neglect were identified in out-patient facilities or in
emergency rooms. Responses to this question indicate that, with
some qualifications, such children were admitted to in-patient facilities in hospitals most accessible to the majority of the population
(87.1 percent). About 14.2 percent of the weighted responses reported no admissions to in-patient facilities; these cases, however,
were referred to other agencies, such as child protection services and
the police. It is significant to note that 2 percent of the weighted answers stated that it depended on what the parents wanted to do; 4
percent admitted the abused children and let the neglected ones go
home, with no mention of reporting to other agencies; and 1 percent
did not know what happened. The modal estimate of the prevalence
of medical and health care needs among children who came to the attention of protection agencies was "more than half" of the cases. Furthermore, of all cases investigated by the police, a weighted average
of 45.1 percent involved children who were taken to hospitals, clinics,
or other health care facilities.

Five groups of respondents (those for child protective services,
public health nursing agencies, school systems, hospital medical departments, and hospital social services) were asked about the services
their respective programs were able to provide or secure for children
and families involved in abuse and neglect. Table 4.17 presents a detailed list of these services; these distributions reflect the specialization of the various organizations. In addition to services provided by
the responding agencies themselves, others were sought from a variety of organizations (Table 4.18).

TABLE 4.17
SERVICES PROVIDED BY FIVE PROGRAMS IN SURVEY SAMPLE

Service	Percentage	Service	Percentage
Marital and family coun-		Child day care services	8.2
seling	22.3	Education services	5.2
Alcoholism counseling	1.3	Special education place-	
Counseling child	15.4	ments	1.9
Counseling parents	15.2	Legal services	5.4
Counseling unmarried		Transportation services	3.7
parents	0.5	Providing volunteers	0.9
General psychological coun-		Parent's group services	2.2
seling	74.2	Care of children	0.6
Counseling foster parents	1.4	School liaison	3.8
Testing and diagnostic ser-		Recreation services	2.4
vices	12.3	Services for handicapped	0.7
Medical exam or check-up	5.2	Placement services	11.7
Nutrition and diet services	9.2	Foster homes	12.4
Birth-control information	2.3	Group homes	1.1
Nursing service	24.0	Treatment facilities	0.4
Home visits by public health		Adoption service	0.3
nurses	5.0	Other placement facilities	2.0
Alcoholism treatment	1.6	Supervision in home	23.5
Medical aid	43.4	Investigation	10.1
Other medical services	0.6	Follow-up services	4.9
Help with child care	8.5	Referrals to other agencies	
Homemaker service	18.7	and services	46.1
Other home-support func-		Referrals to courts	1.1
tions	0.5	Protective services	8.5
Vocational counseling	0.7	Miscellaneous	34.6
Job training programs	2.2	Don't know	4.5
Job placement services	1.7		
Other job-related services	0.6		
Financial assistance	27.9		
Housing	5.7		
Clothing	15.4		
Food	16.2		
Budgeting help	1.6		
Medicaid	2.2		
Other financial services	0.8		

NOTE: Organizations participating in the programs included child protective services, public health nursing agencies, school systems, hospital medical departments, and hospital social services departments.

A persistent source of frustration for workers in this field, and one frequently mentioned during unstructured interviews in a number of communities, was the abusive and neglectful parents and guardians who resisted advice to seek help from mental health clinics, psychiatrists, counselors, psychologists, and similar professions and facilities. To test the prevalence of this problem, three related questions were asked of certain groups of respondents: How often did they recom-

TABLE 4.18
SOURCES FOR SERVICES SOUGHT BY PROGRAMS
IN SURVEY SAMPLE

Source	Percentage	Source	Percentage
Social services	10.3	Housing authority	1.4
Child protective agency	23.4	Outreach programs	0.2
Welfare department	16.7	Other public agencies	3.5
Police department	2.2	Unspecified private agencies	1.2
Probation office	1.4	Churches or ministers	6.9
Courts	2.7	Catholic family services	3.4
Prosecuting attorney's office	0.8	Family service agency	1.4
Hospitals or clinics	8.2	Volunteers	3.2
Hospital social service unit	0.2	Home extension service	2.5
Mental health care facilities	25.0	United Fund or Salvation Army	3.0
Psychological counseling office	5.5	Legal aid	1.2
Drug or alcoholic treatment center	0.4	Private counseling	1.4
Other medical facilities	4.2	Private drug or alcohol treatment	1.1
Public health department	12.8	Day care	1.1
School	4.5	Society for Prevention of Cruelty to Children	0.1
School nurses	0.3	Parents Anonymous	1.4
Special schools—blind, deaf, etc.	0.6	Foster homes or other placement facilities	1.8
School counselors	0.4	Other private agencies	1.7
Parent-Teacher associations	0.2	Social workers	0.4
Colleges, universities	0.7	Physicians	5.2
Child abuse team or SCAN team	0.9	Psychiatrist or psychologist	1.8
Vocational rehabilitation office	1.1	Lawyers	0.2
Mental retardation agency	0.9	Miscellaneous	5.2
Community action office	0.9	None	0.9
Veterans' Administration	0.1		

mend that parents seek such help? How often did they find them
reluctant to seek the help? and How helpful did respondents believe
the services were to those who used them? Answers to these questions are included in Table 4.19. The majority of weighted responses
recommended these types of services "almost always" or "often."
Still, it was surprising to see how many responses from hospital personnel (medical as well as social services) indicated that mental
health services were "hardly ever" recommended to abusive and neglectful parents. This may be due, however, to the concentration, in
the hospital setting, on medical treatment for the children; hospital

TABLE 4.19
RECOMMENDING MENTAL HEALTH SERVICES TO PARENTS
AND GUARDIANS

	Organizations and Responses			
Questions and Responses	CPS	PHN	HMD	HSS
How often are mental health services recommended?				
Almost always	27.0	36.7	44.3	33.8
Often	44.2	24.4	16.5	18.3
Sometimes	19.8	12.6	6.0	15.6
Occasionally	7.7	9.7	8.3	8.5
Hardly ever	1.3	9.1	23.2	23.3
Not applicable* or don't know	0.0	7.6	1.8	0.5
How often do parents or guardians show reluctance to seek help?				
Almost always	8.5	12.4	16.4	13.1
Often	42.1	37.0	24.7	25.5
Sometimes	34.2	16.6	11.8	17.8
Occasionally	9.9	11.5	9.4	6.0
Hardly ever	2.8	1.8	6.3	7.6
Not applicable* or don't know	2.5	20.7	31.4	30.1
How helpful are the services?				
Very helpful	28.2	33.4	22.6	33.3
Somewhat helpful	68.7	0.0	43.6	35.6
Little help	0.0	40.9	0.0	0.0
No help	0.0	4.9	0.0	0.0
Not applicable* or don't know	3.1	20.8	33.8	31.0

*"Not applicable" refers to weighted responses indicating that no services were
recommended.

personnel may tend to rely on other agencies more in contact with parents to deal with the parents' problems.

Reluctance on the part of parents and guardians to avail themselves of mental health services seems to be widespread (Table 4.19). It was "almost always" or "often" the case in more than half the weighted responses for all agencies where the question was raised. The modal answers for all organizations except public health nursing agencies were that these services were "somewhat helpful." Public health nurses representing about half the population felt that such services offered "little help." It should be noted that, of all respondents, public health nurses are probably in the best position to assess the effectiveness of the mental health services received.

"One of the difficulties in dealing with child abuse is that the parents may know they are abusing the child but they are afraid to go to official government lest they be charged with a crime or their children be taken from them."[1] This, and the belief that persons who have experienced similar problems are more apt to extend greater understanding and assistance, led to the emergence of "Parents Anonymous" groups (patterned after Alcoholics Anonymous) in various parts of the country. A series of questions was incorporated in the survey inquiring about the existence of such groups in the sampling communities, asking whether respondents' agencies refer parents and guardians to them, and requesting an evaluation of the influence of participation in them. Considering that personnel from child protective services should be most knowledgeable about the existence of such groups, figures in Table 4.20 would indicate that they were constituted in communities including slightly more than a third of the U.S. population. The least awareness of parents' groups was expressed by hospital medical personnel. The majority of weighted responses indicated that, when such groups were available, the agencies surveyed made referrals to them. Most reasons for nonreferral were based on a preference that child protective agencies undertake this task, if it is necessary, or on "lack of knowledge" about the parents' groups themselves. Although the great majority of weighted responses from all agencies indicated a belief that these groups would help those who joined them, there was a significant proportion of dissenting opinions. Most skeptical were respondents from school

TABLE 4.20
SELF-HELP GROUPS: AVAILABILITY, REFERRAL, AND ASSESSMENT

Questions and Responses	Organizations and Responses					
	CPS	PHN	SCH	HMD	HSS	CRT
Do Parents Anonymous or similar groups exist in community?						
Yes	35.1	33.0	26.1	15.4	30.3	27.7
No	62.1	50.5	68.3	74.9	64.1	53.4
Don't know	2.8	16.5	5.6	9.7	5.7	18.9
Does agency refer parents to these groups?						
Yes	31.2	23.2	18.6	11.3	19.3	14.0
No	4.0	9.0	7.4	3.8	10.2	12.7
Don't know or none exist	64.9	67.8	74.0	84.9	70.5	73.3
Do you feel these groups would be helpful?						
Yes	95.6	82.2	71.0	79.8	86.2	76.3
No	0.9	14.6	22.5	11.7	8.7	9.1
Don't know	3.6	3.2	6.5	8.5	5.1	14.5

systems, public health nurses, and hospital medical personnel, in that order.

Respondents from the five agencies most involved in the delivery of services were asked whether there were any services needed by abused and neglected children or their families that were unavailable or difficult to obtain. Affirmative answers ranged from a high of 84.8 percent for protective agencies to a low of 38.5 percent for hospital medical personnel (Table 4.21). Public health nurses, who are also involved in mobilizing community services for their clients, were second to protective agencies in the prevalence of affirmative responses (70.5 percent). Variations in assessing the availability and accessibility of services partially reflect the agencies' differing orientations—some are more child-oriented, others are parent-oriented, and still others are family-oriented. In this respect, greater confidence must be placed in the responses of protective services personnel, since it is their primary responsibility to manage cases of abuse and neglect through the maze of available and desirable services.

This analysis was pursued further by comparing communities

where there was a consensus that services were lacking with others where the consensus was that needed services were available and accessible. The attempt was to derive some characterization of communities with inadequate services. The results show that such communities are larger and tend to have more cases of abuse and neglect. It is also apparent that communities with no coordination and those with case management coordination show a far lesser degree of service unavailability than those with only administrative-level coordination.

Respondents to the question about service availability were also asked to name the specific types of services that were inaccessible to them or impossible to obtain. Table 4.21 presents a detailed listing of these services. Although counseling seems the service most often unobtainable or difficult to obtain, home support, such as homemaker services or child care, is also frequently mentioned. Other services named by respondents from agencies representing significant proportions of the population include financial assistance and child placement facilities. In some ways, the responses reflect differences in the agencies' roles. For example, child protective service personnel often cite suitable placement as difficult or impossible to obtain, whereas physicians, who seldom undertake responsibility for placement, are less likely to mention this problem. The same can be said for such services as financial-assistance and home support. Finally, it is particularly important to note the proportions of the population residing in areas where agencies found that needed medical and other health care services were impossible or difficult to obtain for abused and neglected children.

One of the most crucial decisions in intervening with problems of abuse and neglect is whether to remove children or to leave them with parents and guardians who have mistreated them. These decisions will be the subject of further analysis later in this study; however, it is important to discuss here the considerations entailed in such decisions and their bearing upon the provision of services. These considerations include the effects of removal to unfamiliar environments, especially upon young children; the adequacy of placement alternatives and their potentially disruptive influence on family relations; and the attitudes and reactions of parents, particularly the

TABLE 4.21
SERVICES IMPOSSIBLE OR DIFFICULT TO OBTAIN

Service Availability	Organizations and Responses				
	CPS	PHN	SCH	HMD	HSS
Are any services impossible or difficult to obtain?					
Yes	84.8	70.5	60.6	38.5	53.9
No	14.1	29.5	38.4	54.8	42.8
Don't know	1.1	. . . .	1.0	6.6	3.3
Types of service impossible or difficult to obtain					
Marital and family counseling	8.1	1.5	7.2	5.8	4.1
Alcoholism counseling	0.6	. . . .	. . . .	. . . .	. . . .
Counseling for child	3.5	3.2	2.3	3.6	4.0
Counseling for parents	4.2	1.1	1.6	9.5	4.2
General psychological counseling	33.9	33.3	39.1	37.8	26.7
Testing and diagnostic services	3.1	0.8	0.9	7.9	4.0
Medical exam or check-up	1.3	. . . .	. . . .	. . . .	. . . .
Nutrition and diet services	. . . .	1.9	0.2	0.6	3.4
Nursing	3.2	8.8	6.8	0.4	2.1
Birth control information	. . . .	0.3	0.6	. . . .	. . . .
Home visits by public health nurses	. . . .	. . . .	0.4	. . . .	3.1
Alcoholism treatment	0.2	. . . .	0.6	. . . .	0.5
Medical aid	8.1	8.7	15.7	2.5	3.5
Other medical services	. . . .	0.6	. . . .	1.1	0.4
Instruction on child care and help with children	4.1	4.0	1.1	7.3	3.2
Homemaker service	22.8	14.0	5.7	3.3	15.7
Other home support functions	5.2	0.1	. . . .	2.5	. . . .
Vocational counseling	. . . .	. . . .	. . . .	0.1	. . . .
Job training programs	. . . .	. . . .	. . . .	0.7	3.4
Job placement services	4.8	. . . .	1.8	0.1	0.4
Other job-related services	0.6	1.4	. . . .	. . . .	3.1
Financial assistance	10.7	10.2	5.1	8.7	16.0
Providing housing	12.3	6.5	3.7	2.6	8.1
Providing clothing	0.3	. . . .	2.8	. . . .	0.3
Providing food	. . . .	. . . .	1.8	. . . .	0.3
Budgeting help	1.8	0.5	0.6	1.2	3.8
Other financial services	0.6	1.6	. . . .	. . . .	. . . .
Day-care services	13.3	8.3	0.4	8.2	18.6
Education services	0.5	0.7	3.9	2.9	4.2
Special education placement	6.7	1.0	3.5	. . . .	1.2

Service Availability	Organizations and Responses				
	CPS	PHN	SCH	HMD	HSS
Types of service impossible *or difficult to obtain*					
Legal services	3.4	0.4	2.3	0.5	1.7
Transportation services	5.6	7.9	3.9	3.6	11.2
Providing volunteers	6.2	. . . .	1.4	0.4	3.1
Parent's group services	3.7	5.9	4.7	6.4	14.3
School liaison	1.6	. . . .	0.7	. . . .	. . . .
Recreation services	4.3	. . . .	. . . .	1.1	0.5
Services for handicapped	2.1	1.5	1.0	. . . .	0.2
Placement services	5.1	. . . .	2.0	0.9	0.5
Foster homes	3.1	9.1	7.7	3.0	3.9
Group homes	3.8	. . . .	0.1	0.2	0.4
Treatment facilities	5.4	0.6	0.1	. . . .	2.1
Other placement services	10.5	3.0	6.2	1.8	1.9
Supervision in home	. . . .	0.3	1.0	1.5	2.4
Investigation	0.7	. . . .	0.1	. . . .	. . . .
Follow-up services	. . . .	0.8	1.7	8.8	2.7
Referrals to other agencies and services	1.4	. . . .	4.7	0.2	1.3
References to courts	. . . .	1.9	2.9	4.1	. . . .
Protective services	. . . .	1.7	2.0	4.9	1.3
Miscellaneous	4.8	17.2	21.1	16.5	19.8

NOTE: Column totals may exceed 100 percent because of multiple responses.

damage to potential counseling or therapeutic relations that could be developed with professional workers. Any deliberation on these decisions, however, assumes that priority will be given to the protection of children from the risk of further abuse and neglect.

A criticism frequently leveled against child protection agencies is that, because of their caseworkers' desire to maintain rapport with parents or because of limitations in staffing and resources, children are often left with parents in spite of continued abuse and neglect.[2] In order to arrive at some estimate of the prevalence of these practices, we asked respondents from child protective agencies about the proportion of parents and guardians who continued to abuse their children after the agencies became involved; the proportion of parents and guardians who continued to neglect their children after the agencies became involved; the proportion of children who had been part of their active caseload and who suffered continued abuse and neglect requiring hospital treatment; and the proportions of cases who had been part of their caseload and who came to the attention of the police because of continued abuse and neglect.

Responses to these four questions are presented in Table 4.22, which demonstrates a number of significant trends. Only a third of the population lives in areas where child abuse continues in "almost none" of the cases after protective agencies become involved. The corresponding weighted responses for neglect account for only 8.8 percent of the population. It is no more reassuring to note the propor-

TABLE 4.22
CHILD PROTECTIVE AGENCY ESTIMATES OF CONTINUED MALTREATMENT
AMONG THEIR ACTIVE CASES

Proportions of Cases	Victims Suffered Continued Abuse	Victims Suffered Continued Neglect	Victims Were Taken to Hospital	Victims Became Known to Police
Almost all	2.3	3.2	2.1	7.8
More than half	3.0	8.9	4.3	10.7
About half	8.9	29.9	12.2	10.9
Less than half	45.0	40.0	38.7	39.6
Almost none	33.3	8.8	40.0	26.1
Don't know	7.5	9.2	2.6	5.0

tions of cases in the active caseloads of protective agencies that were subsequently taken to hospitals for treatment or that came to the attention of the police because of continued maltreatment. In order to verify information obtained from child protective agencies on this issue, respondents from hospital medical and social service staff were asked about the proportions of abuse and neglect cases brought to their hospitals which had been part of the active caseloads of protective agencies. Respondents from police and sheriff's departments were asked similar questions about the proportions of such cases among those that came to their attention. These estimates (Table 4.23) corroborate the widespread presence of continued abuse and neglect serious enough to merit medical treatment or the involvement of the police.

The estimates of continued child abuse and neglect just presented should become important in decisions concerning the removal of children or in the development of other ways to assure their protection. They also constitute revealing indicators of the effectiveness of the services provided by the child protective agencies, as well as those services the agencies were able to obtain from other sources in their communities.

TABLE 4.23
HOSPITAL AND POLICE ESTIMATES OF CONTINUED MALTREATMENT
AMONG CASES SERVED BY CHILD PROTECTIVE AGENCIES

Proportions of Cases	Victims Taken to Hospitals for Treatment		Victims Became Known to Police
	HMD Estimates	HSS Estimates	
Almost all	6.2	6.7	14.6
More than half	10.5	12.6	23.0
About half	14.7	18.6	17.6
Less than half	9.6	18.5	15.1
Almost none	41.6	27.8	21.4
Don't know	17.4	15.7	8.2

Other indicators of the adequacy of child protective services were sought by asking about the sufficiency of current resources, as well as priorities in the use of new funds, should any become available. A recent GAO study reports that while federal authorizations for child welfare services under Title IV-B programs have increased from $55 million in 1968 to $211 million in 1974, the Department of Health, Education, and Welfare has never requested appropriations of more than $47.5 million.[3] The same report shows that these appropriations do not represent the total expenditures on these services, which were estimated to have reached over one billion dollars, of which the federal share was about $683 million during the fiscal year 1972. Child protective agencies seem to have remained short on funds and resources. As shown in Table 4.24, 89.1 percent of the weighted responses from these agencies reacted affirmatively to an opinion item stating, "Agencies are not given sufficient resources to deal effectively with child abuse and neglect." Distributions of responses from other agencies also indicate an overwhelming sense of the insufficiency of resources. Agreement with this statement ranged from 72

TABLE 4.24
REACTIONS TO OPINION ITEM:
"AGENCIES ARE NOT GIVEN SUFFICIENT RESOURCES TO DEAL
EFFECTIVELY WITH CHILD ABUSE AND NEGLECT"

Reactions	Organizations and Responses						
	CPS	PHN	SCH	HMD	HSS	CRT	POL
Strongly agree	56.1	39.1	43.2	31.4	45.1	29.8	45.9
Tend to agree	33.0	42.3	48.6	41.1	38.1	42.2	29.8
Tend to disagree	7.0	13.5	6.2	15.4	12.8	22.2	15.7
Strongly disagree	3.3	3.3	0.7	3.5	2.3	1.9	4.7
Don't know	0.6	1.8	1.2	8.5	1.7	3.9	3.9

percent for respondents from the courts to 91.8 percent for those from school systems.

Further specification of the need for resources and of their priorities was sought by asking respondents from the various agencies: "If additional funds were to become available to your agency for child abuse and neglect, what are the most important uses you would like to see these funds put to?" It was requested that uses be ranked in order of importance. Responses to this question (Table 4.25) were grouped under the following categories: "Personnel," which refers to increasing staff in respondents' agencies or adding specialists in certain fields; "Improved Staffing of Other Agencies," which would

TABLE 4.25
USES FOR ADDITIONAL AGENCY RESOURCES

Priorities	Organizations and Responses						
	CPS	PHN	SCH	HMD	HSS	CRT	POL
Personnel	72.4	58.5	64.7	46.7	55.0	46.5	57.7
Improved staffing of other agencies	8.6	23.4	13.8	19.4	15.4	17.5	17.1
Intraagency operations	42.8	38.3	37.6	25.1	34.4	22.8	41.1
Placement facilities	49.1	21.1	20.5	15.8	27.4	46.7	25.7
Services/programs in community	75.1	56.1	50.6	48.3	56.2	41.9	26.3
Services to other agencies	45.4	42.1	22.6	32.7	42.0	23.7	38.0
Interagency functions	12.3	13.3	9.9	7.4	13.3	2.0	12.5
Miscellaneous	16.9	35.8	21.6	25.0	21.3	16.6	37.7
None	1.9	9.0	5.8	18.5	10.8	18.2	10.3

NOTE: Column totals may exceed 100 percent because of multiple responses.

require increasing staff numbers or improving qualifications and training; "Intraagency Operations," which would include such things as adding specialized divisions or sections, adding 24-hour coverage, improving information retrieval, and so on; "Placement Facilities," which would mean providing such things as foster homes, emergency and temporary facilities, and half-way houses; "Services and Programs," referring to services such as homemaking, nutritional education, volunteer programs, and counseling; "Services Available to Other Agencies," which would require increasing legal,

TABLE 4.26
COST ESTIMATES (IN DOLLARS)

Priorities	Organizations and Responses						
	CPS	PHN	SCH	HMD	HSS	CRT	POL
Personnel	123,403	22,638	196,841	9,269	18,686	49,798	17,830
Improved staffing of other agencies	620	12,454	73	....	....	2,077	97
Intraagency operations	5,989	18,145	6,364	740	2,637	251	16,568
Placement facilities	120,230	1,786	1,188	1,093	1,189	18,589	9,182
Services and programs in community	32,402	43,166	39,840	26,845	35,028	12,057	22,679
Services to other agencies	6,181	2,558	3,360	1,141	2,183	5,404	7,794
Interagency functions	590	4,856	1,103	253	313	134	2,723
Miscellaneous	2,389	28,958	3,865	321	3,525	23,412	10,008

medical, social, and/or referral services "Interagency Functions," which would mean establishing multiagency teams, coordinating committees, and other forms of liaison; "Miscellaneous" responses, which did not fall within any of the first seven categories; and "None," indicating neither needs for resources nor priorities expressed.

Distributions in Table 4.25 clearly reveal that the greatest need in each of the agencies is for personnel. Additional resources would be utilized to strengthen internal programs, as well as to make services available to other agencies. As will be discussed later, child protective agencies and the courts emphasized the need for placement facilities. The low mention of interagency functions was not a reflection of strong existing liaisons. The need for stronger interdependence among agencies was indicated by the more frequent mention of "services available to other agencies."

Respondents were asked to estimate the cost of providing for needs they indicated, should additional funds become available. Since respondents for many agencies did not supply the necessary cost estimates, the sheer aggregation of costs mentioned would be misleading. In this analysis an average cost for each of the eight categories used in grouping needs was estimated for each agency or program. The results are shown in Table 4.26. The average cost of increasing the numbers or improving the quality of personnel in child protective agencies, for example, is slightly over $120,000 per agency; the corresponding figure for school systems was almost twice as much (about $200,000). The total costs are highest for child protective services, followed by schools. It is interesting to note that hospital pediatric departments were least in terms of needs for additional resources, followed by police.

It must be noted, however, that these estimates are crude and entail considerable overlap across agencies. For example, protective agencies, the courts, and the police allocated considerable funds for the development and improvement of placement facilities. Also, public health nursing departments assigned high costs to improving the staffing in other agencies. Another source of instability in these figures is the high nonresponse rate on requests for cost estimates; this might be largely attributable to the fluid situation in regard to child maltreatment problems. The ability to make cost projections is limited by the respondents' uncertainty about the appropriate size for their caseloads. Thus respondents who firmly perceived the need for staff expansion might not have been able to anticipate the additional manpower needed, and so could not estimate its cost.

In spite of these limitations, the cost estimates are instructive in some respects. For example, the allocations for "staffing other agencies" seem to indicate that the inadequacies of current personnel in some agencies were keenly felt in others. And the average cost estimates given by child protective agencies permit a useful distinction to be made between one-shot expenditures, such as those for placement facilities ($120,230), and the regular operating costs represented by the other items ($171,574). This means that estimates of needed resources for all of the 129 such agencies included in the survey would amount to about $15.5 million in one-shot appropriations for placement facilities and about $22 million in additional annual operating costs. Considering that the jurisdictions of these 129 agencies include about a third of the U.S. population, the national projections of these agencies' needs for additional resources would be $46.5 million in cost of facilities, and $66 million in annual appropriations for program operations.

Finally, another significant indicator of the quality of services is the level of knowledge and skills characteristic of available personnel.

TABLE 4.27
STAFF ATTENDANCE AT CONFERENCES AND WORKSHOPS

	Organizations and Responses						
	CPS	PHN	SCH	HMD	HSS	CRT	POL
None attended	2.3	23.5	29.7	39.4	24.6	20.6	32.5
Attended within last year	88.3	67.7	57.9	38.9	62.0	63.2	56.7
1–5 years ago	7.4	7.9	9.8	16.8	12.8	7.5	10.7
Don't know, other	2.0	0.9	2.6	4.9	0.7	8.7	0.2

The collection of specific data about staff qualifications in these organizations was beyond the scope of this study. Nevertheless, some information about participation in workshops, conferences, and other meetings addressed to the problem of child maltreatment was sought. In this respect, respondents were asked, "When was the last time any of the staff attended any program dealing with child abuse?" Answers to this question are included in Table 4.27. Child protective agencies reported the most frequent recent attendance, hospital medical personnel and the hospital social services the least. A sizable proportion of the population is represented by agencies from which someone has attended such programs within the six-month period preceding interviews for this study. It is still important, however, to note the low level of attendance at such programs by most agencies, especially by members of hospital pediatric departments. It should be added also that in many of the agencies the persons attending training programs were frequently heads of departments or supervisors.

LEGAL INTERVENTION:
CUSTODY AND PLACEMENT

Abraham Katz's position on the legal rights involved in parent-child relations and the state's right to intervention constitutes a useful framework for the presentation of survey data on these issues. He maintains (as mentioned earlier) that, while "the state places a high priority on a stable and independent parent-child relationship," it imposes upon parents specific responsibilities toward their children—"financial security, health, education, morality, and respect for people and authority."[4] Clearly, each of these responsibilities represents a continuum, and the state's right to intervene is invoked in cases of failure to meet what is considered minimum necessities along the range of parental responsibilities.

The process of intervention begins with reports of abuse and/or neglect, followed by investigations conducted by authorized agencies. Often, children are permitted to remain in their homes, and services are provided to them and their parents. These three phases in the state's intervention process—reporting, investigating and providing services—were discussed in earlier sections of this report. In many cases, however, the state's intervention takes legal form, whether or not services are needed or provided. The following section presents data related to legal intervention and its consequences, as organized under five headings: process of legal intervention, change of custody, placement of children, reuniting children with their parents, and follow-up practices.

Legal Process

Beyond a report or an investigation by authorized agencies, Katz views as legal intervention challenges to parents' right to custody, court investigations, or court hearings.[5] Table 4.1 presents the relative frequencies with which affidavits concerning abuse and neglect are filed by various sources to the courts. These distributions show that the most frequent sources are child protective services, offices of prosecuting attorneys, welfare services, police and sheriff's departments, and relatives, in that order.

In cases involving the emergency removal of children from their homes, the time given the involved agencies to obtain a court authorization ranged from within 24 hours (46.3 percent), to within one week (31.3 percent), and even to more than a week (1.3 percent). In courts representing 18.4 percent of the population, court orders were always required prior to removal. The rest of the respondents did not know about time limitations for court authorization of emergency removal. Respondents from the courts were also asked how often court orders actually were obtained prior to the temporary removal of children. Their answers, in percentages, were:

Always	1.9
Almost always	34.4
Often	11.8
Sometimes	16.8
Occasionally	11.7
Hardly ever	20.3
Don't know	3.1

In courts representing the great majority of the population (83.5 percent), judges made the decisions about petitions for temporary removal. For 8.2 percent of the population, decisions were made by court referees and for 14.7 percent by other officials.

TABLE 4.28
RATES OF COURT REFUSAL FOR TEMPORARY REMOVAL PETITIONS

Rates of Refusal	As Reported by Courts for All Petitions	As Reported by CPS for Their Petitions	As Reported by Police for Their Petitions
Almost always	....	....	1.4
Often	....	....	....
Sometimes	13.4	6.7	16.3
Occasionally	20.2	38.8	29.2
Hardly ever	64.6	54.5	49.7
Don't know	1.9	....	3.4

The rates of court refusals of these petitions are summarized in Table 4.28. In addition to estimates of refusal for all of the petitions given by respondents from the courts, the table presents a comparative picture of these rates for petitions made by child protective agencies and the police. The table reveals that courts tend to refuse petitions emanating from the police slightly more often than they do those from protective agencies. In order of frequency, "lack of evidence and inability to show cause," "the court is feeling that removal was not in the best interest of the child," and "improper petitioning procedures" were the reasons given by respondents from the courts for refusing petitions advocating the temporary removal of children.

Respondents from the protective agencies were asked several questions concerning the availability of legal assistance. Over 40 percent of the population resides within jurisdictions whose protective agencies reported receiving "all" the assistance they needed from the offices of prosecuting, city or county, or state attorneys. Furthermore, agencies representing 52.5 percent of the population either employed lawyers or retained them, and an additional 10.5 percent of the weighted responses mentioned the occasional use of consultants. This rate of coverage (and perhaps its quality) seems seriously inadequate for these agencies' legal aid needs. When asked if they felt that their agencies' work was "hindered in regard to child abuse and neglect because of inadequate legal assistance," affirmative answers were given by respondents from agencies serving 50.9 percent of the population. Respondents described such impediments as: long waits for legal advice; their own inability to prepare adequately for court procedures and hearings; errors caused by ignorance of the laws and of the alternatives available to agency personnel; bias in the legal aid available to them, often in favor of parental rights; and incompetent legal counseling.

Of all the cases of abuse and neglect brought to the attention of the courts, estimates of the percentages resolved without formal court hearings were as follows:

Almost all	6.5
More than half	15.0
About half	19.7
Less than half	17.1
Almost none	29.4
Don't know	12.4

Cases more likely to have been resolved informally were described as "less serious," "more of neglect than abuse," and those in which "parents were cooperative in taking voluntary actions to alleviate the problems." The most commonly mentioned approach to informal resolution was to delegate the responsibility for working out appropriate arrangements to child protection or other social service agencies, which would then inform the court. The second most common approach was for court personnel to make investigations, arrangements with the families, and recommendations to the respective judges. In courts representing over one-fourth of the population (29.0 percent), judges determined whether or not a case proceeded to formal hearings. In the rest of the courts, various people were empowered to make such decisions; responses included other personnel in the courts (especially "intake" and probation officers) and other agencies (especially child protective services). Among the characteristics associated with the cases most likely to proceed toward formal hearings were abuse—especially when serious—chronic maltreatment, lack of cooperation from parents, and sufficient evidence for legal action.

TABLE 4.29
LEGAL REPRESENTATION OF PARENTS

Frequency of Representation	In Informal Resolutions	In Formal Hearings
Almost always	21.1	63.0
Often	7.2	11.9
Sometimes	18.9	15.0
Occasionally	19.1	6.6
Hardly ever	29.7	3.4
Don't know	3.7	. . . .

Respondents from courts were asked "how often parents were represented by lawyers" in both informally resolved cases and in formal hearings. As might be expected, estimates presented in Table 4.29 indicate a much greater preponderance of legal representation in formal hearings. In fact, in courts representing 28.3 percent of the population, lawyers were assigned to cases when parents could not afford such representation. Courts representing 20.6 percent of the population never appointed a guardian *ad litem* to represent the interests of children in formal hearings. Such appointments were reported with the following frequency distributions:

Almost always	40.5 percent
Often	6.9 percent
Sometimes	8.2 percent
Occasionally	12.8 percent
Hardly ever	11.0 percent
Never	20.6 percent

When the appointment of a guardian *ad litem* was the practice, lawyers predominated as appointees in the ratio of nearly four to one. In a descending order of frequency, nonlawyers appointed to this role included relatives, representatives of social agencies, probation officers, and others.

Table 4.30 tallies the types of evidence acceptable to the courts in abuse and neglect cases; many of these actually constitute dimensions that would be very useful in attempts toward the further speci-

TABLE 4.30
TYPES OF EVIDENCE ACCEPTABLE TO COURTS

Types of Evidence	Abuse Cases	Neglect Cases
Testimony of lay witnesses	36.9	33.9
Testimony of expert witnesses	14.6	37.3
Testimony of physician	29.1	10.4
Testimony of child	9.2	9.3
Condition of child	22.2	18.4
Delinquency of child	1.2	1.3
Truancy of child	0.0	5.2
Health records	41.6	23.7
Other tangible evidence	25.3	31.1
Evidence that child is unsupervised	1.6	18.3
Evidence that child does not get medical attention	0.8	7.2
Evidence concerning child's lack of necessities	0.0	4.8
Testimony or evidence concerning parents' behavior	8.4	2.2
Evidence of physical or emotional damage to child	7.9	3.2
Circumstantial evidence	5.2	5.7
Hearsay evidence	3.1	1.6
Same types of evidence acceptable in any court	2.7	1.2
Anything relevant	2.4	3.4
Anything relevant except hearsay	2.3	2.3
Other	4.1	6.6

NOTE: Column totals may exceed 100 percent because of multiple responses.

fications of criteria. The distributions indicate a greater tendency to rely upon medical and health-related evidence and testimonies in abuse cases, whereas expert witnesses (other than physicians) and evidence concerning child supervision assume relatively more significance in neglect cases. The distribution of witnesses who appeared in formal court hearings (Table 4.31) indicates that reliance was most frequently placed upon personnel from child protective agencies, followed by police witnesses, hospital physicians, and relatives, in that order.

TABLE 4.31
WITNESS DISTRIBUTIONS IN FORMAL COURT HEARINGS

Types of Witnesses	How Often Do They Appear?					
	Almost Always	Often	Some-times	Occa-sionally	Hardly Ever	Don't Know
Protective service personnel	78.8	9.6	2.4	5.4	3.2	0.6
Hospital physicians	11.9	14.8	24.1	22.0	25.8	1.4
Hospital social workers	7.9	11.3	22.8	15.1	42.1	0.7
Physicians in private practice	4.6	12.2	17.5	20.0	45.0	0.6
Police	19.7	27.9	33.3	10.9	7.5	0.6
School officials	5.9	14.0	39.8	29.2	10.6	0.6
Public health nurses	4.7	14.1	22.9	22.2	35.5	0.6
Relatives	9.6	36.0	27.7	19.1	7.0	0.7
Friends and neighbors	3.7	17.5	39.8	24.6	13.8	0.7
Others	27.7	29.5	18.2	19.0	5.6	....

NOTE: Column totals may exceed 100 percent because of multiple responses.

According to respondents from the courts, the latter were most likely to remove children from their homes if they felt the children would be in danger at home, if they perceived removal to be in the children's best interest, if parents were uncooperative and refused to seek help, or if parents were unable to care for the children. It is important to note that not all formal court hearings involve petitions for change of custody. Respondents from courts representing only 30.5 percent of the population mentioned that such hearings always involved challenge to parental custody. In order of importance, other issues that became involved in formal hearings in the remaining courts included authorizing the supervision of child protective agencies, requiring parents to seek mental health treatment, requesting temporary custody, and requesting the return of children to their parents. Respondents from courts with jurisdictions representing 88.9 percent of the population reported that parents "occasionally" or "hardly ever" appealed decisions reached in formal hearings.

The data presented so far characterize the legal processes involved in the challenge of parental custody: the court's investigation in terms of evidence and testimonies, informal resolutions, and formal hearings. One resulting conclusion is that this process tends to be less formal in smaller communities than in those with larger populations. Furthermore, in spite of the presumably nonadversary nature of the courts involved, legal representation is frequent, especially in connection with formal hearings. From the point of view of distributive justice, it is important to consider differentials in the ability to secure legal representation, as well as the effects of such representation and the likelihood of appeals upon the disposition of cases. Valid opinions on these subjects would have been difficult to obtain through a survey of the practices and opinions of those already in charge of court decisions. Information obtained through unstructured interviews, however, as well as studies in similar decision-making processes lead to the conclusion that differences in the availability of legal representation and the threat of appeals do introduce varying degrees of influence upon court decisions. Some may consider this an indication of unequal justice favoring parents at higher socioeconomic levels. Others may view the inequality from the perspective of the socioeconomically favored children who are clearly disfavored in maltreatment cases because of the legal facilities available to parents who may be abusive or neglectful.

Change of Custody

Estimates of the final dispositions of cases requiring formal hearings, presented in Table 4.32, designate the proportions of abuse and neglect cases that resulted in the termination of parental rights to custody, in temporary changes in custody, and in no changes in custody. Although legal distinctions between abuse and neglect are not necessarily maintained in all courts, this did not create any difficulties in classification for this survey. As would be expected, both permanent and temporary changes in custody were less prevalent in cases of suspected neglect than in those of abuse. The termination of parental custody frees the children for adoption. Except for the possible appeal of such a disposition and the provision of adoption services, the involvement of public agencies in such cases also comes to a close. In the majority of cases, however, there was either no change or only a temporary change in custody.

Respondents were asked a series of questions about court requirements and actions in decisions involving custody (Table 4.33). The most frequently mentioned requirement is counseling or therapy. Im-

TABLE 4.32
CUSTODY DECISIONS IN FINAL DISPOSITIONS

	Abuse (percentages)		Neglect (percentages)	
Dispositions known to respondents	83.8		88.3	
Termination of parental custody		19.5		15.8
Temporary change of custody		44.4		42.2
Children not removed from home		19.9		30.3
Dispositions not known to respondents	16.2		11.7	

provement in interpersonal relations, the physical conditions of the home, and home supervision were also mentioned in significant proportions of the weighted responses. Supervision was required more often when children were left at home, the responsibility most frequently being delegated to child protective agencies, followed by probation departments.

Respondents from courts representing 3.7 percent of the population reported that parents were not allowed to see their children when there was a temporary change of custody. In the remaining jurisdictions, if parents were allowed to contact their children after removal, child protection agencies were most likely to determine or participate in specifying the nature of contacts (84.2 percent), followed in frequency of mention by the probation departments and others connected with the courts (46.1 percent).

Temporary Placement

Of all the respondents in this survey, the personnel of child protection agencies were expected to be most knowledgeable about the temporary placement of abused and neglected children for whom a

TABLE 4.33
COURT REQUIREMENTS FOR PARENTS

Court Requirements	Status of Children	
	Temporarily Removed	Left at Home
Proportion of cases requiring probation or supervision		
Almost all	36.0	53.7
More than half	14.2	12.1
About half	7.2	8.2
Less than half	5.1	4.6
None or almost none	36.5	19.2
Don't know	0.9	2.3
Supervisors for parents' compliance		
CPA or other social service personnel	74.7	67.3
Probation department	44.0	27.8
Other	14.7	4.9
Don't know	. . . .	. . . .
Typical requirements for compliance		
Counseling or therapy for parents	67.8	33.6
Improvement in domestic inter-personal relations	16.3	14.8
Physical improvement in home	19.0	18.9
Ceasing abuse or neglect of home	5.0	6.1
Other improvements in home	2.7	1.9
Home supervision	11.6	15.9
Medical follow-up	5.8	7.0
Attendance at meetings	7.6	7.4
Curfew	2.6	1.9
Restrictions on drug or alcohol use	7.1	9.0
Change in attitude	0.8	3.0
Cooperation with court	9.2	17.9
Supervision by a social agency	4.7	9.1
Other	8.9	12.4
Don't know	0.3	4.9

NOTE: Column totals may exceed 100 percent because of multiple responses.

change of custody had been authorized. Several questions were asked of these respondents about the types of facilities used, their quality, and other problems encountered in placement. Data on the types of facilities and their usage (Table 4.34) indicate that the majority of children were placed in foster homes, although placement with relatives was the second most frequently employed resource. Agencies representing slightly less than a quarter of the population also mentioned the use of detention homes. These facilities were utilized mostly for teenage children and those with "behavioral problems," for "delinquents or pre-delinquents," or for "neglected" children. Decisions on such placement were made by judges, caseworkers, probation officers, and the police, with fairly similar rates of prevalence.

TABLE 4.34
ESTIMATES OF TYPES OF PLACEMENT

Estimated Percentages	Types of Placement			
	Foster Homes	Relatives	Detention Homes	Other Facilities
None	2.3	1.0	75.8	55.2
1–25	12.1	66.4	15.7	31.5
26–50	18.1	25.9	5.3	5.8
51–75	26.1	0.9	1.0	1.6
76–100	35.5	1.6	0.6	0.1
Don't know	5.9	4.3	1.5	5.8
Average Percentage	65.0	21.1	4.4	6.8

The existence of facilities other than foster homes, relatives, and detention homes was reported for communities including about half of the population sample (50.3 percent). These included children's shelter homes (25.3 percent), group homes (16.5 percent), treatment facilities (12.4 percent), orphanages (7.3 percent), runaway homes (6.6 percent), and similar types.* In most cases where such facilities existed, their use was not limited to the placement of abused and neglected children. As implied by their names, their residents included delinquents, children with physical and mental impairments, runaways, and others who for a variety of reasons became dependents or needed custodial care. Finally, it should be noted that the results of the survey indicate that hospitals were at times "used as a place to keep children who were temporarily removed from their homes when

* The cumulative percentages for the facilities exceed 50.3 because some communities had several types of facility.

[hospitalization] is not medically necessary." This practice, however, seems to be fairly limited.

In general, the importance of any care that substitutes for that of parents and families cannot be over-emphasized, especially for younger children. The need for high-quality care is even greater when children are removed from their homes under conditions of abuse and neglect. And yet evidence gathered in this study indicates that temporary placement is one of the weakest aspects of services and intervention programs. Conflicts in the professional roles of case-workers in protective services have been outlined earlier. These conflicts are based on the differing needs and interests of multiple clientele: the abused and neglected children; the abusive and neglectful parents and guardians; and foster parents, especially aspirants for adoption. It should be added that our data revealed the potential for such conflicts to be quite widespread, since child protective agencies representing 80.1 percent of the population also handled foster home placement themselves.

It is unrealistic to expect foster parents to develop the emotional commitment necessary for the desired quality of care when agencies emphasize the temporary nature of their relations to the children involved. Katz illustrates other aspects of the problem:

> From a theoretical perspective, foster care is designed to be a non-permanent arrangement, and as a consequence, standards for choosing temporary custodians differ from those for permanent custodians. Experience has shown that to assume non-permanence in foster care is unrealistic. Children placed in foster care remain in that status longer than is generally admitted by many placement agencies. Yet some agencies . . . . continue to hold foster parents and children in a state of limbo while jealously guarding biological ties. Their protection of the natural parent's rights often represents a misplaced loyalty and is sometimes simply a rationalization for the agency's own decisions.[6]

Evidence also indicates that children were frequently moved from one foster home to another, and that two or more moves per year were not uncommon.[7] This was done not only with teenage children, whose personal incompatibilities may lead to the need for change, but also occurred for infants under 2. No explanations are available for this pattern, which deserves careful study. Still, regardless of the underlying reasons, the important question concerns the effects of such instability upon the children. Finally, it must be noted that, considering the numbers of children in foster homes, the rates of abuse and neglect attributed to foster parents looms significant (Table 3.3).

Responses in the present survey demonstrate that, for 75.9 percent of the population, child protection agencies encountered difficulties and delays in placing children in foster homes. For 65.3 percent of the population, the difficulty was primarily one of shortage. The rest attributed the trouble, at least in part, to certain characteristics of the children needing temporary placement, particularly behavioral problems and physical or mental impairment. Finally, when respondents from the courts were asked to assess the quality of available facilities for temporary placement in their jurisdictions, their appraisals were: good (44.3 percent), adequate (38.2 percent), poor (15.2 percent, and 0.1 percent) did not know. Those who rated these facilities as less than good were also asked about the problems and limitations characteristic of their communities. The most widely mentioned problem was the lack of sufficient foster homes and other facilities, followed by limitations in the quality of those available. Frequently mentioned and important was the shortage of facilities appropriate for handling short-term crisis situations. In summary, both the survey results and the unstructured interviews conducted in a number of communities highlighted the difficulties in temporary placement, a major issue in serving abused and neglected children.

Reunition and Follow-Up

For the majority of the population (76.3 percent), the duration of temporary change in custody was determined by the courts in consultation with other agencies, primarily the child protection and social services. For 14.5 percent of the population, these decisions were made by the courts independently. For the remaining 9.2 percent, decisions involving temporary custody did not involve the courts. It is important to note variations in estimates expressed in percentages, of the average duration of temporary custody:

Up to one month	5.3 percent
Two to three months	18.1 percent

Four to six months	22.1 percent
Seven to twelve months	19.3 percent
Over one year	6.2 percent
Don't know	29.0 percent

Some cases were reported to last several years. Of significance also is the high prevalence of "don't know" responses to this question (29 percent). Although respondents for court jurisdictions, including close to half of the sample (48.9 percent) felt that the duration of temporary custody was associated with certain characteristics of the children involved as well as with given attributes of parents and guardians (48.7 percent), the only clear agreement concerning these characteristics is that children under 5 experience temporary custody for longer periods.

The conditions most likely to have persuaded child protective agencies and the courts to return abused and neglected children to the custody of their parents included indications of improvement in the home situation, progress in counseling and/or a change in the attitudes of parents, and the availability of services and follow-up plans. Within child protection agencies, decisions concerning the return of children were made most often by the caseworkers themselves (44.5 percent), and slightly less often by heads of agencies and supervisors (43.9 percent). Respondents from child protection, public health nursing, and hospital social service agencies, reported that their organizations and programs provided follow-up services when abused and neglected children were not removed from their homes, and often also when families were reunited. The average durations of these services were 7.7 months, 10.3 months, and 4.5 months for the three types of agencies respectively. As would be expected, the most prevalent consideration for terminating follow-up by any of these three was "the improvement and stabilization of the family condition." Caseload pressures were also among the factors affecting the duration of follow-up by protective services. Finally, it is of interest to note that protective agencies serving 11.3 percent of the population and courts representing 20.6 percent had no involvement in returning any abused or neglected children to their families during the year prior to interviews.

DECISION MAKING

The identification and management of child abuse and neglect cases requires that service and law-enforcement personnel make many decisions which could create serious risks for affected children and parents. Such decisions include whether to report suspected cases, whether to investigate reports, whether to leave the children in the custody of potentially or actually abusing and neglectful parents and guardians, how to select appropriate placement for children removed from their homes, how to provide or arrange for needed services for children and parents, how to reunite families, whether to extend or to terminate follow-up services, and whether to terminate parental custody and free the children for adoption. The process of decision-making is built around the development of criteria, the collection of evidence, and the exercise of judgment in applying criteria to evidence and reaching a decision. The decision-making structures concerning child abuse and neglect vary not only among communities, but also from one agency to another within the same community. Such variations have considerable bearing upon the quality of the decisions made. Justice and effectiveness require that decisions be fair and equitable, and that they serve the best interests of abused and neglected children. Often, however, these decisions are influenced by factors extraneous to the problem. Some of the potential sources of bias will become evident as we first examine the important issues involved in the elements of decision making.

Criteria

Determining whether a child has been abused or neglected or whether a parent has been abusive or neglectful immediately raises the question of criteria, that is, the indications upon which one bases such distinctions. In complex phenomena such as abuse and neglect, distinctions and determinations are often based upon multiple criteria, which must balance diverse and conflicting interests. The development of conceptually and methodologically defensible indices, which combine the relative weights of the various dimensions of abuse and neglect, remains one of the pressing areas of needed research.

Attempts have been made, and progress has been achieved, in the development of criteria and other operational indicators for physical abuse and neglect based primarily upon medical and other health conditions. Unfortunately, the same cannot be said for other types of abuse and neglect, or for such related questions as, What determines fitness for parenting? What are the mimimum standards? How can healthy development be ascertained? What constitutes appropriate child care? As mentioned earlier, the status of the development of criteria reflects current substantive and technological limitations in the field. Fifty-six percent of the weighted responses from child protective agencies, and 64 percent from police departments agreed with the statement, "it is difficult to say what is and what is not child maltreatment," so did even higher proportions of the weighted responses of judges and physicians. There were even greater rates of agreement with the statement, "it is difficult to determine when parents should have their children returned." Proportions of the population served by agencies responding affirmatively to this statement ranged from 68 percent for the courts to 86 percent for hospital medical personnel.

In varying degrees, all concepts exhibit openness of meaning; that is, there is a potential variation in the correspondence between the meaning a term such as *abuse* or *neglect* acquires and actual case-by-case observations and decisions by users of the term. It is often difficult to decide "whether or not something belongs to the designated class," so that "belongingness in any case is a matter of degree."[8] The problem of "where to draw the line" arises not only in identifying the categories of children to whom the terms *abuse* and *neglect* apply, for example, but also in distinguishing subclasses of children on the basis of the types and degrees of abuse and neglect inflicted. There is always the possibility of borderline cases, wherever the lines may be drawn. To be aware of open meanings for crucial concepts and terms and to recognize vagueness around the lines of differentiation, is not, however, to sanction apathy and carelessness. Rather, the purpose is to emphasize one of the major problems underlying difficulties in the delivery of services and the administration of justice in this field. Identifying a problem is a step toward addressing it.

Evidence

What constitutes evidence may vary with the context or purpose for which it is used. In common, everyday situations evidence may be anything that persuades the mind that a given factual proposition is true. In law, however, evidence designates facts that meet the requirements set by certain legal rules. These rules govern the nature of admissible facts and specify the methods by which facts are to be established.

Subjectivity enters into evidence in at least two major ways. The first involves the process of selecting facts. Contrary to the popular saying, "facts" do not speak for themselves; they must be conscientiously sought out and assembled. They are selected from a wide range of observations and the selection rarely, if ever, can be said to be complete. Evidence selection requires a number of subjective decisions. To note that evidence can be selected is one issue, but the basis for selecting among various possibilities is another. Some caseworkers, police officers, and agency personnel interviewed in depth mentioned early "impressionistic decisions" as guides for their selection of evidence. In other words, decisions seem to be made on the basis of impressions. Once such decisions are reached, the evaluation or investigation searches for evidence to document them. Needless to say, this is the reverse of the optimal process of decision making, in which the collection of evidence is guided by the criteria identifying the problem, with judgments and decisions deferred until evidence has been gathered and examined.

Subjectivity also enters evidence through opinions and interpretations. The rules of evidence in the Anglo-American system of legal and administrative proceedings have generally excluded "hearsay" and "opinion," confining a witness to describing what he or she perceives, and thus reserving the function of inference to the jury, or to the judge or evaluator. "Only an expert qualified to the satisfaction of the court may testify to the inferences he drew from his perceptions."[9] The problem of distinguishing between perceptions and conclusions, however, is not always easily resolved. Even the "nonadversary" procedures of courts handling abuse and neglect cases are open to the opinions and interpretations of police officers, caseworkers, physicians, and other sources of information. Furthermore, subjectivity may enter not only into oral testimonies, but written reports as well, especially those in narrative form.

Important as they are, issues involved in evidence have generally received little research attention. The objectives of research and development efforts in this area should be to facilitate the collection of evidence and to develop its utility. Within this context, the utility of evidence is a function of its relevance, that is, the degree to which it is related to both the phenomenon being evaluated and the criteria of evaluation; its accuracy in representing the facts, that is, its freedom from errors of identification and measurement; its timeliness, or its correspondence to current conditions; and its adequacy, that is, its completeness.

Judgment

The role of judgment in decisions varies according to the specificity-diffuseness of criteria and the nature of evidence. Two types of decision process can be identified. First is a process based upon objectively defined criteria for which there are concrete indicators, as in determinations concerning the eligibility of widows for certain insurance benefits. Such decisions are of a routine nature, and only entail the mechanical matching of simple evidence with clear-cut criteria.[10] Sometimes, when the items of evidence called for are not available, designating an acceptable substitute may create difficulties, but the disposition of these problems has also become fairly routinized. Decisions of this type require not only that specific criteria be established, but also that relative weights be accorded to each. To make such decisions, only evidence related to established criteria need be collected.

The second type of decision process, which may be termed nonroutine, entails judgment on the meaning of criteria, the relative weights they are to be assigned, the nature and relevance of evidence, and the application of criteria to evidence. Typical nonroutine decisions are based upon an inductive process in which broadly categorized data may be relevant and necessary. In this process, one looks for signs, trends, syndromes, and clues, which would then require further review of the data to determine their significance. The extent to which "meaning" is derived from the data may depend as much on the artfulness of the decision makers and the constraints placed upon them, as on the nature or extent of the data.

These two decision models represent a continuum. As the phenomena about which decisions are made become better understood and their indicators more clearly delineated, routinization of decisions becomes more feasible. At present, most, if not all, major decisions concerning abuse and neglect are much closer to the nonroutine end of the continuum. The susceptibility of these decisions to the subjective influence of human judgment raises a number of questions about the disposition of doubtful cases. It is a truism to assert that decisions in doubtful cases are more likely to be subject to errors in judgment than cases representing obvious extremes. To illustrate, a doubtful case may be determined to involve abuse when "in fact" it does not, or not to involve abuse when "in fact" it does. Similarly, a case may be determined to require certain action (e.g. change of custody) when "in fact" it does not, or not to require such action while "in fact" it does. These two errors—concluding that a given condition exists, when it does not, and that a given condition does not exist, when it does—are usually referred to as false positives and false negatives, respectively. Without further specification of the meaning, the identifying criteria, and the nature of evidence, attempts to limit the false negatives would almost automatically result in an increase in the false positives, and vice versa.

This dilemma raises important issues in decisions concerning the identification and control of abuse and neglect. To begin with, there is the question of the consequences of each of the two types of decision errors for children and for parents. While one type of error constitutes a risk for the children's safety and well-being, the other entails undue harassment of parents. Since the absence of clear-cut criteria and evidence in nonroutine decisions leads to an increase in doubtful cases, another important issue concerns the rules or norms that guide judgment in such cases. For example, the general norms in medicine are to minimize the false negatives, even if it means an increase in the false positives. This is consistent with the provision of medical care, and therefore, "most physicians learn early in their training that it is far more culpable to dismiss a sick person than to retain a well one."[11] On the other hand, the norm in law is that "a man is innocent until proven guilty." Here the emphasis is upon minimizing false positives and acquitting defendants unless the judge or jury "find the evidence of guilt compelling beyond a reasonable doubt," the rationale being that "the individual is . . . weak and defenseless, relative to society, and therefore in no position to sustain the consequences of an erroneous decision."[12]

Inferences that can be made from the findings of this study would lead to the conclusion that there are no consistent decision rules in regard to these problems. They vary according to agencies, to professional backgrounds, and quite frequently to individuals. Wide differences in informal decision rules were reflected in responses to a question about the degree to which personnel in the respective agencies varied in "decisions and approaches to problems of abuse and neglect." The answers are presented in Table 4.35. Responses citing "no" variations ranged from 13.9 percent for personnel in child protection agencies to 77.4 percent for those in hospital social services. On the other hand, reports of "great" variations were highest among medical personnel (37.3 percent) and lowest among those from hospital social service agencies (2.2 percent). As might be expected, "some" variations were reported by agencies representing large proportions of the population.

TABLE 4.35
ESTIMATED VARIATIONS IN CASEWORKER DECISIONS

Degree of Variation	Organizations and Responses						
	CPS	PHN	SCH	HMD	HSS	CRT	POL
Great	20.6	12.2	21.2	37.3	2.2	14.4	4.3
Some	65.5	61.2	53.2	43.4	20.4	60.7	39.8
None	13.9	26.6	25.6	19.3	77.4	24.9	55.9

As mentioned earlier, equity, fairness, and effectiveness in programs are predicated on error-free decisions, and especially on decisions free of errors of a systematic nature that tend to impede service or law-enforcement efforts. One way to limit variations in judgment and other related subjective influences is to move the decision process toward the routine end of the continuum. Such change can only be accomplished through further specification of criteria and evidence, however, and at present there is much room for improvement along those lines. Furthermore, as has already been mentioned, opinions will always exert some degree of influence over decisions concerning such complex issues as those emanating from cases of abuse and neglect. Because of this, it is necessary to examine approaches that involve the structure of decision making.

Structure

Generally, three structural approaches have been used in attempts to reduce the subjectivity of decisions. The first is due process, which is oriented to achieving the norms of justice in judicial decisions. Its basic element is the right to be heard before a decision is taken that affects one's life, liberty, or property.[13] Bernard Schwartz explains that the right to be heard should include the right to be heard orally; to present evidence and argument; to rebut adverse evidence through cross-examination and other appropriate means; to be bound only by decisions based solely upon known evidence; and to appear with counsel.[14] Furthermore, as the Supereme Court declared in 1968, the right to a jury trial is granted to criminal defendants "in order to prevent oppression by the government . . . and to provide . . . an estimable safeguard against the corrupt or overzealous prosecutor and against the compliant, biased or eccentric judge."[15] Neither court hearings concerned with abuse and neglect nor other related procedures adhere to either of these structural approaches—due process or jury trial. The arguments against introducing them assert that they would interfere "with the informal 'helping' nature of the courts and violate the principle of *parens patriae*."[16] Hence, as Sanford Katz points out,

> Hearing procedures vary from jurisdiction to jurisdiction. Generally, however, the hearings are informal and private. Unlike criminal proceedings, which are governed by strict rules of evidence, neglect hearings tend to allow for wide-ranging inquiries beyond the specific allegations of neglect. . . . Many jurisdictions give wide discretion to the judge, allowing him to make whatever disposition he deems will advance the child's best interests. Others limit the judge's discretion to actions short of legally terminating the parent-child relationship.[17]

Further increasing the openness of court decisions in regard to abuse and neglect is the vagueness of statutes governing parent-child relations. One judge observed:

> The neglect statutes are concerned with parental behavior, not as behavior per se, but only and solely as it adversely affects the child in those

areas of the child's life about which the statutes have expressed concern. Each child embodies his own unique combination of physical, psychological, and social components, no child has quite the same strengths or weaknesses as another or exactly the same relationship with his family. The parental failure which markedly damages one child might leave another quite untouched. This interaction between the child and his family is the essence of a neglect situation, the imponderable which defies statutory constraints.[18]

Katz maintains that "it is the nonspecific statute which provides the judge with a vehicle for imposing on others his own preferences for certain child-rearing practices and his own ideas of adult behavior and parental morality."[19] Equally important are the false negatives and false positives inevitable in court decisions when open to individual judgment. As mentioned earlier, such errors entail substantial risks for children and parents, especially when they concern custody, and even more when permanent separation is at stake. In conclusion, we believe that due process remains a viable and important option.

The second approach of public agencies in addressing subjectivity in decisions is to place them in the hands of "professionals," who presumably possess specialized knowledge and skills relevant to the problems at hand. There is a paradox here, however, since the fact that decisions are open to the exercise of judgment indicates that knowledge concerning the problems is both incomplete and nonspecific. The following excerpts on police decision-making in regard to the "unprotected child" illustrate the paradox:

Juvenile personnel are selected for specialization partly on the basis of demonstrated decision-making in other areas of police work, along with other considerations regarding qualifications. . . . Of all police branches, juvenile enforcement can least afford an officer who is incapable of making solid decisions that can stand the test of time. . . .
. . . Many departments have no established policy guidelines for the officers to follow in the application of police discretionary power. The officer is sent forth to analyze the situation, and only after he has taken action will the "second guessing" begin. . . . If, as most professionals argue, such policies cannot be set down in writing because of the individuality of each case; then it must be conversely stated that the officer, when making a bad decision on an individual case cannot be expected to learn from his own experience, as the case is individual and unique. . . .
The truth is, no policy is written because there is not enough knowledge

and understanding of the basis of police decision-making at this time to form a foundation for the establishment of adequate policy.[20]

Arguments have been advanced that caseworkers in child protective agencies are better prepared professionally to handle initial investigations.[21] The distinct impression gathered in field interviews, however, was that the rate of turnover in these positions is high, resulting in less cumulative experience. Furthermore, it was often mentioned that the current training of social workers does not equip them to handle decisions of this type appropriately. It is thus no accident that personnel was one of the highest ranking areas of need in child protective agencies, and that upgrading personnel quality was a prevalent concern—nor were these responses (Table 4.25) unique to protective services. The central issue, however, continues to be whether the available knowledge and technology are sufficiently developed to provide the basis for decisions free of personal bias and other extraneous influences. And, it need hardly be added, the literature abounds with indications of such influences in "professional" decisions.[22]

A third approach in guarding against the consequences of subjectivity is to favor "group decisions"—those made by two or more persons. These persons could be from the same agency or from different agencies; similarly, they could have the same professional background or could represent different professions. While some view interdisciplinary "team" approaches as a panacea, others regard them as accomplishing nothing more than compounding the ignorance of individual participants. Neither extreme presents a constructive position.

If properly managed, collective views, especially if they represent diverse professional perspectives, are less likely to be influenced by subjective or extraneous factors. The findings of this survey, however, indicate that individual decisions prevail in current practice. For example, in protective agencies representing about 60 percent of the population, caseworkers themselves make decisions to seek temporary custody; in agencies responsible for 42 percent of the population, they also make decisions to seek permanent separation or return of children to their families. Furthermore, reports from police departments serving 61 percent of the population indicate that the officer on the scene makes decisions on the removal of children from their homes. Changes in the decision-making structure toward collective and interdisciplinary forms would not only require change in the internal procedures within given agencies, but much closer coordination of programs as well.

PROGRAM COORDINATION

In this analysis the term *program* is used to designate those service and law enforcement activities directed to the control of child maltreatment or to the alleviation of its consequences. In this sense, a program is not to be equated with any given agency or organization. Ideally, integrated program planning involves identifying objectives, then selecting methods and technologies appropriate to the objectives, and finally organizing programs to implement these methods. The actual development of child maltreatment programs is far from approximating this ideal pattern.

Like programs addressed to other multiproblem categories, those concerned with child maltreatment have experienced fragmentation—a predictable consequence of agency specialization. Obviously, for one agency to handle all the activities related to child abuse and neglect is neither possible nor necessarily desirable. Nevertheless, the involvement of such functionally specialized agencies as the police, the courts, the hospitals, and the schools inevitably raises the question of coordination. Presumably child welfare and protective agencies were conceived with coordination in mind. Indeed, it is largely because of this intended coordination that Alfred Kadushin found it "difficult to neatly classify protective services" in a scheme categorizing services to families as "supportive, supplementary, or substitutive."[23] But, although the function of protective agencies is to cut across all three types, their lack of authority vis-à-vis other agencies, as well as their limited resources and the limited training and experience of their staff members, have severely reduced their effectiveness in this role.

Emphasis in the literature on coordination has been primarily on the various forms of cooperation among agencies; and exchange framework has provided the most useful perspectives for such analysis. Sol Levine and Paul E. White define organizational exchange as

"any voluntary activity between organizations which has consequences, actual or anticipated, for the realization of their respective
objectives."[24] It should be noted that exchange refers not only to reciprocal activities, but also to organizational activities in general.
Thus, an exchange can be unidirectional, as when one organization
refers a client to another. This broad definition permits consideration
of various dimensions of organizational interaction that might otherwise be overlooked.

Theoretically, if all organizations were endowed with infinite resources, there would be no need for organizational exchange. Given
the actual conditions of scarcity, however, interorganizational exchanges are necessary for goal attainment. The complex network of
agencies concerned with child abuse, for example, can be viewed as
an exchange system, the agencies' interrelationships being determined according to their needs or commitment to the control of this
problem. The elements which are exchanged fall into three basic categories: clients; manpower with various skills; and such nonlabor
resources as funds, information, and equipment.[25] Agencies dealing
with child abuse differ in their needs for these elements according to
their resources and their program functions.

William Reid suggests that the exchange perspective has two ad-
vantages in an analysis of interagency coordination.[26] First, it draws
attention to organizational goals. Any organizational activity, including coordination, may be viewed as directed toward goal achievement, no matter how the organization defines its own goals.

> Viewing coordination as an exchange through which agencies attempt
> to achieve their goals forces consideration of what these goals actually
> are. In this type of analysis, one need not assume that the most impor-
> tant agency goals be in furthering the welfare of the community, or that
> agencies in a community are bound together in a closely knit system in
> which each seeks similar goals through different means. Much of the
> prescriptive writing on coordination assumes that agencies have or
> should have common goals. It is another matter, however, to examine
> agency goals for what they are without prior assumptions or illusions.
> Only in this way can the subject of interagency coordination be dealt
> with analytically.[27]

Second, the exchange perspective brings into focus the importance, in any coordinative activity, of organizational resources, which

may be broadly defined as any elements an organization needs to achieve its goals. An exchange among organizations can be described in terms of the types of resources included in the transaction.

Using a typology based on the extensiveness of the exchange, Reid delineates three levels of coordination that hold a great deal of promise for analyzing the relationships among agencies involved in child protection programs. The first, *ad hoc* case coordination, is least costly and does not require extensive organizational commitment. The following are instances of this level of coordination: a physician in a hospital attempts to obtain social services for a family in which he suspects child abuse; a teacher tries to get a public health nurse to visit the home of a child she suspects is being maltreated; or a caseworker in a child welfare agency introduces a parent involved in child abuse to a local unit of Parents Anonymous. These examples illustrate an unstructured or emergent exchange process, as opposed to service integration, which occurs when organizations have a general policy of working together in certain types of cases and have established rules for handling them. This second level of exchange represents a more formal interorganizational relationship and is less dependent upon the idiosyncrasies of the functionaries involved. The third level of coordination, program integration, is reached when two or more organizations establish special programs, jointly coordinated and managed, to accomplish goals common to both participating agencies. The institutionalization of such programs represents greater commitment to goals and greater assurance of continuity.

Mechanisms for controlling the exchange relationships are also significant. Reid maintains that shared goals and complementary resources are often sufficient conditions for lower levels of coordination, such as the *ad hoc* type, if agencies have mutually respected domains. For more systematic forms of coordination, however, formal means of control must be developed. "Such control mechanisms," as Reid notes, "may take the form of interagency agreements, of regularly scheduled case conferences between staff members of different agencies, or interagency committees. Program coordination may require such mechanisms as formal agreements, accountability procedures, interagency conferences, and allocations of coordinating responsibilities to specific staff members."[28]

One of the mechanisms for controlling exchange among agencies concerned with child abuse has been in the form of the interagency committees which serve as central clearinghouses or coordinators of related agencies, and occasionally as catalysts in the development of new services.[29] At times, the work of such committees may extend beyond program coordination to the actual handling of cases. The impetus for the development of interagency committees may come not only from the personnel of certain public or private agencies, but also from concerned citizens, who may take part in the committees once they are formed.

Another approach to the control of organizational exchange is through coordinating agencies, which have as their objective the ordering of "behavior between two or more other formal organizations by communicating pertinent information, by adjudicating areas of dispute, by providing standards of behavior, by promoting areas of common interest, and so forth."[30] This type of agency attempts to coordinate independent organizations either because they have conflicting goals or because, although they share common goals, the demands of efficiency dictate specialization. Examples of coordinating agencies would involve only higher administrative levels. It should be noted that, at the level of day-to-day delivery of services, the coordinating agencies' control of exchange has not been effective. And the involvement of varying jurisdictional levels—federal, state, local, and voluntary—further reduces the effectiveness of the coordinating agencies as mechanisms for controlling exchange in regard to the problem of child abuse.

Complex interagency coordination is both costly and difficult. Thus agencies "are often reluctant to devote expensive staff time and other resources to less than adequate regulation of complex exchanges. Unless commitment to shared goals and need of complementary resources provide sufficient force, agencies may decide that coordination is not worth the price."[31]

Finally, the distinction should be made between interdisciplinary and interagency coordination. Interdisciplinary coordination occurs when a team of members from different professions and occupations, nevertheless function as a unit within one organization. This pattern can be found more frequently in hospitals and mental health clinics than in any of the other agencies concerned with child maltreatment. Typically, such teams include physicians, nurses, case workers, and other volunteers or professionals. Interagency coordination, on the other hand, links independent organizations. As observed earlier, the linkage varies in formality and occurs at various levels—it can occur, for example, at the policy and general level or in day-to-day case management. The number and types of agencies entering into coordinative agreements also vary, of course, from one community to another.

Guided by the previous conceptual distinctions, several questions on formally organized interagency coordination in the sample areas were included in this survey. Table 4.36 presents the types and prevalence of coordinative arrangements as reported by respondents from the various agencies. Although differences in responses largely reflect the pattern of participation in and knowledge of such arrangements, they may also, to a lesser degree, reflect differences in terminology. Since protective agencies are the most central for programs addressed to child maltreatment, and therefore the most likely to know about coordinative activities and to take part in them, more reliance can be placed upon their information.

Depending upon the reporting agency, 55.6 percent to 76.8 percent of the population lived in areas where there were no centers for action on child abuse and neglect, no interagency teams, and no liaison committees or other mechanisms for interagency coordination. Nonparticipation in interagency linkages, where such linkages existed, was highest for the courts (7.7 percent) and lowest for public health nurses (1.4 percent). Protective services representing 2.5 percent of the population reported the existence of liaison activities in which they took no part.

The coordinating bodies varied in composition, function, and administrative location. In the majority of cases, when these bodies had been established they included four or more participant agencies. Department heads and supervisors, not lower-level staff, most commonly took part in coordinating efforts. This may indicate that most coordinating efforts were directed toward interorganizational relations rather than actual case management, since emphasis on the latter would require the participation of police officers, caseworkers, nurses, and others directly engaged in the delivery of services. The fact that teams and liaison groups generally met only once a month also indicates more concern with general matters than with day-to-day case management.

TABLE 4.36
PATTERNS OF INTERAGENCY COORDINATION

Patterns of Coordination	Organizations and Responses						
	CPS	PHN	SCH	HMD	HSS	CRT	POL
What are forms of coordination?							
Teams	24.0	14.4	15.6	12.3	14.7	15.4	19.7
Centers	0.9	2.5	0.9	1.1	1.1	0.6	2.3
Liaison committees	19.3	18.5	7.6	5.6	7.6	13.5	5.0
Other mechanisms	0.2	0.1	1.5	....	1.6	2.1	0.4
None	55.6	64.2	72.5	76.8	71.1	66.4	71.6
Don't know	....	0.2	2.0	4.2	4.0	2.0	0.9
Does agency participate?							
Yes	41.8	34.2	22.3	14.3	20.3	24.5	23.9
No	2.5	1.4	3.7	4.5	5.6	7.7	2.7
No coordination in community	55.6	64.4	73.9	80.1	74.0	67.8	72.4
Don't know	....	....	....	1.1	....	....	1.0
Who participates?							
Administrators	19.9	3.3	13.3	6.3	13.5	12.9	12.0
Personnel at operating level	22.6	30.5	9.8	7.0	11.0	13.7	12.5
No distinction could be made	....	....	....	2.1	0.3	....	....
No coordination in community	57.4	66.2	77.0	83.9	75.2	73.4	75.5
Don't know	....	....	....	0.6	....	....	....
How many agencies participate?							
Only one	1.1	0.4	2.3	5.0	4.6	1.0	1.1
Only two	2.2	1.0	1.8	2.4	2.7	3.0	2.0
Three	8.1	4.1	3.0	2.9	2.0	3.7	2.5
Four	2.9	6.0	2.6	2.6	4.2	6.5	4.0
Five or more	30.0	23.6	14.6	5.9	13.4	15.1	15.6
No coordination in community	55.6	64.2	73.1	77.1	70.4	67.1	72.4
Don't know	....	0.7	2.6	4.1	2.6	3.6	2.4
Are records kept in common pool?							
Yes	2.7	7.6	1.9	4.8	2.5	2.5	3.4
No	41.0	26.5	19.9	10.4	21.3	21.6	21.7
No coordination in community	56.2	65.5	77.8	83.9	75.0	74.8	74.4
Don't know	....	0.4	0.3	0.9	1.3	1.1	0.4

NOTE: Percentages across questions differ because of varying amounts of missing data, which are not included in tables.

A close examination of responses concerning the nature of interorganizational liaisons revealed that about 15.6 percent of the population resided in jurisdictions reporting a case-management level of coordination; and an additional 28.8 percent, in jurisdictions characterized by liaisons concerned with other forms of "administrative" coordination not involving case management. The remaining 55.6 percent of the population were in areas where the working relations among agencies reached neither level of coordination. In order to test the relationship between these three forms of relations (case-management coordination, administrative coordination, and no coordination) and interagency difficulties, respondents were asked if the ways other agencies handled cases of abuse and neglect caused delays or other problems for the respondents' respective agencies.

Table 4.37 presents the weighted proportions of agencies in the survey, according to the three levels of coordination, that experienced such problems in their relations with three or more other agencies. A consistent curvilinear relationship was revealed, for every agency, between levels of coordination and the prevalence of problems. This indicates that the development of coordination in child maltreatment programs follows three broad transitional phases. The first phase is characteristic of communities where there are no pressures for coordination. Because agencies operate in an independent manner, no problems exist concerning roles, boundaries, control over resources, or control over clientele. Thus these agencies tend to perceive fewer problems in relating to each other than do those in communities where pressures toward coordination exist.

The second phase involves agencies in the early stages of developing coordinative mechanisms. Since the perception of needs for coordination generally stems from heightened awareness of the problem, it is not surprising that programs in this phase have exhibited the most interagency difficulties. Even if no coordination exists, awareness of the problem and of the need for interagency relationships can be in itself a source of considerable dissatisfaction. The problem is further compounded by apprehensions about roles, responsibilities, and boundaries, as well as concern over the distribution of resources. No doubt the exposure to one another, as potential collaborators on serious decisions, of personnel with varying disciplinary and professional backgrounds adds to their anxiety and sensitivity concerning interagency difficulties.

The third phase, that of close coordination and actual case management, occurs when most of the difficulties involving boundaries and responsibilities have been resolved. Generally, personnel from the various agencies have become acquainted with one another's orientations and approaches. Because this phase is characterized by the more precise articulation of roles, it is also marked by a reduction of problems and difficulties in interagency relations.

TABLE 4.37
LEVELS OF COORDINATION AND WEIGHTED PERCENTAGES
OF SURVEYED AGENCIES EXPERIENCING INTRACOMMUNITY PROBLEMS

Levels of Coordination in Communities	Organizations and Responses				
	CPS	PHN	HMD	HSS	POL
No coordination	57.2	22.3	3.0	23.7	23.5
Administrative coordination	77.5	29.3	9.4	36.0	27.8
Case-management coordination	65.9	29.2	5.5	17.8	18.7

The three phases actually represent abstractions of a continuum. But from a "therapeutic" viewpoint at least, the information gathered in this survey should prove useful to communities, especially those in the second phase, working toward program coordination. The implications of these analyses reach beyond programs concerned with child maltreatment, however, and extend to efforts toward coordination around other community problems.

The prevalence of difficulties in interagency relations was also surveyed independently of its relations to levels of coordination. Table 4.38 presents a cross-tabulation of organizations that reported interagency problems and those named as the sources of the problems. Perhaps because of their central role, child protective services experienced more difficulties than any other agency in the survey. Child protective services and hospital medical personnel showed a high level of mutual dissatisfaction, as did the police and child protective services. The schools ranked high on the problem lists of child protective services and the police, while the courts were ranked fairly high as sources of problems by most respondents' agencies. Finally, it

TABLE 4.38
PREVALENCE OF AGENCY PROBLEMS CAUSED BY OTHER AGENCIES

	Agencies Experiencing Problems					
Agencies Causing Problems	CPS	PHN	HMD	HSS	POL	Weighted Average
Police and sheriff's departments	44.9	12.2	7.2	21.0	....	23.6
Hospital social services	40.2	10.3	4.0	....	15.5	19.1
Hospital medical personnel	56.7	17.8	....	43.0	22.1	34.3
Child protective services	....	27.7	18.3	36.2	22.2	25.8
Other welfare services	32.0	18.7	8.3	25.5	13.2	20.2
Schools	57.0	16.4	5.8	10.6	20.0	25.3
Courts	45.8	23.0	16.1	28.5	15.9	26.8
Mental health clinics	51.8	16.0	5.5	12.6	12.1	22.0
Private organizations	33.2	6.8	1.6	4.8	11.4	13.4
Prosecuting attorney's offices	29.5	14.6	7.2	14.8	9.0	15.9

NOTE: Column totals may exceed 100 percent because of multiple responses.

should be noted also that child protective services were frequently, and in a fairly consistent manner, viewed as sources of problems.

To conclude this section, in Table 4.39 we present data on the nature of the problems and difficulties encountered by the respondents' agencies. This information was obtained in response to the question, "Considering the various facets of the problem, and the many agencies involved, what difficulties do you see in the way child abuse and neglect is handled in this area?" The distributions of responses demonstrate the prevalence of problems and difficulties such as noncentralized handling and lack of interagency cooperation. Insufficiency or inadequacy in staffing, in case identification and reporting, and in placement facilities were also among the most prevalent sources of problems for the various agencies.

TABLE 4.39
PROBLEMS AND DIFFICULTIES IN THE AREA

Problems and Difficulties	Organizations and Responses						
	CPS	PHN	SCH	HMD	HSS	CRT	POL
Insufficient or inadequate staff	33.1	17.6	20.4	8.4	12.9	23.4	16.6
Insufficient or inadequate placement facilities	12.5	3.9	2.0	3.1	3.1	18.0	11.5
Insufficient or inadequate reporting, identification	17.3	28.1	19.1	20.8	21.5	18.0	15.2
Problems in investigating and evidence	0.0	2.9	4.1	1.5	4.4	7.9	1.7
Delays in handling	0.0	8.0	7.4	3.0	1.4	0.9	0.0
Insufficient funds	6.6	10.8	5.5	3.7	1.8	5.2	0.3
Lack of staff training	15.4	7.8	8.9	13.2	9.8	3.9	10.2
Poor public education	16.5	12.9	10.9	12.1	12.9	7.8	10.3
Noncentralized handling	28.7	29.3	10.2	13.9	17.4	7.6	12.0
Lack of interagency cooperation	16.1	25.8	14.2	11.2	16.8	6.1	12.9
Lack of referral agencies or of some services	3.0	4.0	1.8	5.9	4.8	2.7	2.5
Legal limitations	2.3	1.9	2.7	1.1	2.3	4.3	1.0
Courts too slow/lenient	3.0	5.8	5.7	9.0	7.9	2.8	10.9
Reluctance to take child from parents	0.0	4.3	1.3	3.1	2.1	1.2	2.1
Lack of counseling	0.3	2.0	5.4	8.2	2.3	3.3	5.9
Lack of follow up	0.0	10.3	5.5	10.9	3.4	4.7	0.0
Need for community resources	4.7	2.1	2.6	1.8	3.4	6.2	0.0
Need for prevention program	0.0	2.0	4.9	1.1	0.4	0.3	0.0
Complaints about courts	2.4	1.3	4.6	2.6	2.5	4.9	7.2
Complaints about police	0.0	3.0	2.3	0.9	1.9	1.1	0.0
Complaints about hospitals	0.9	0.4	0.5	0.3	0.4	0.8	0.5
Complaints about social service agencies	0.5	3.2	13.0	2.5	3.3	12.7	6.7
Complaints about schools	0.1	0.3	1.0	0.0	0.6	1.2	0.0
Complaints about medical personnel	1.4	1.2	0.7	0.8	3.3	0.0	0.3
Other	25.4	17.2	16.4	7.8	9.0	10.9	8.9
Don't know	2.0	1.5	2.3	5.6	7.3	4.9	2.0
None	5.0	4.3	6.2	13.2	8.2	20.5	21.0

NOTE: Column totals may exceed 100 percent because of multiple responses.

CHAPTER FIVE

TOWARD
ENHANCED
COPING

ONE OF THE primary objectives in this work was to prepare a set of recommendations and to develop a model for the organization of programs addressed to child abuse and neglect. As mentioned earlier, in this report *program* refers to the sum of services,
law enforcement, and other activities brought to bear upon the prevention, identification, treatment, and control of these problems. The
literature abounds with prescriptions, ranging from specific instructions for professionals and others on "how to do it," to admonitions,
addressed to society at large, to renounce violence and distribute
wealth more equitably. Between these extremes of specificity and
breadth exist a host of opinions and conclusions concerning needed
program components, required educational and support activities,
and improved organizational patterns. A few of these recommendations are well reasoned and grounded in the realities of the problem; some have been important sources of information and suggestions for this work.

Appraisals of the practices and performance of various agencies
and programs pervade this entire report. While risking repetition, we
believe a concluding assessment would be useful, not only to bring
into view a profile of the strengths and limitations of current programs, but also to explicate the basis for the recommendations that
follow. We also believe that such a summary can best be presented in

conjunction with an optimal set of objectives for programs on child maltreatment.

SUMMARY ASSESSMENT

Criteria for evaluating programs are generally derived from their goals and objectives. Hence the ultimate criteria for programs addressed to the problem of child maltreatment are indications that the problem has become less prevalent and/or severe and that intervention has proved effective. In view of the current status of definitions and criteria for identification, however, as well as the levels of knowledge concerning incidence and prevalence, attempts toward assessing the present magnitude of the problem would be futile. And direct evaluation of interventive programs would require specific information about children and parents. Even then, it might be difficult to place a value on programs that help children at the cost of depriving parents or that assist parents but endanger the welfare of children.

These limitations do not mean that appraisals of programs on child maltreatment are impossible, for important inferences can be made in relation to more specific intermediate goals. At concrete and specific levels, goals often resemble means or program functions; they also become more amenable to the development of manageable evaluation criteria. The following are statements of the goals for child maltreatment programs considered in planning this study:

Provision of primary preventive services through both public education and the identification of risk populations, so that potential victims can be reached before maltreatment occurs.

Identification and referral of victims to appropriate agencies.

Intervention in diffuse crisis situations before they become seriously damaging to the children and their families.

Achievement of a balance between deterrent and therapeutic services, remembering that the primary objective of programs is protection rather than prosecution.

Separation of children from their homes, when this is necessary for their protection, and their placement in homes or facilities that will enhance their recovery from maltreatment.

Provision of services to children and/or parents and families, whether the children remain at home or are separated.

Provision of information and training to related professionals, program administrators, and government policy makers.

Provision of decision-making structures commensurate with the seriousness and multidimensionality of the problem.

Provision of effective coordinating systems for agencies, to promote the delivery and continuity of services and the legal handling of cases and to minimize interagency conflict.

The application of these program objectives or functions to the findings of this study, and to others, leads to the following assessments:

First, most efforts toward public education thus far have been primarily to increase awareness of the occurrence of maltreatment, especially of abuse, and to encourage the reporting of such cases when they occur. Undoubtedly, through coverage in the mass media and through public programs, the visibility of the problem has increased greatly over the last ten years. An increase in the visibility of a problem is not always accompanied, however, by an increase in the dissemination of preventive information. Nor does the present state of epidemiological knowledge allow for the identification of risk populations on whom preventive efforts might be concentrated. In fact, knowledge about what would constitute primary prevention is yet to be developed.

Second, if our estimates of the confirmable rates of prevalence of abuse are within an acceptable margin of error, then it can be said that in 1972 the nation was slightly less than halfway to identifying all confirmable abuse cases, and less than one sixth of the way in identifying all confirmable neglect. Frequent failure to report suspected cases was cited by child protective services and by the police for most of the potential sources. Especially problematic, however, were schools, which are in a good position for case identification, and professionals in private practice, especially physicians. Only 16.2 percent of the population resided in areas where the reporting of suspected maltreatment reached or exceeded 17 per 1,000; according to our estimates, this would be necessary to identify 75 percent of confirmable abuse under current laws and practices. And only 4.9 percent resided in areas where reporting reached or exceeded 25 per 1,000, sufficient to identify 90 percent of such cases. In summary, the picture of identification and reporting is highly varied in different areas of the nation, but jurisdictions comprising a clear majority of the population (72.4 percent) are reporting at levels below 10.5 per 1,000, the level sufficient for identifying 50 percent of the abuse cases confirmable under existing laws and practices.

Third, the pattern of responses to reports of abuse and neglect indicates that intervention in crisis situations is largely left to the police, who often reach troubled homes sooner than the personnel of child protective services and public health nurses. Much has been written about differences in approach between the law-enforcement oriented police and the therapeutically oriented members of the other two agencies. Personnel shortages account in part for the inability of protective services personnel and public health nurses to respond to crises more promptly. Furthermore, when reports made to police and sheriff's departments are investigated, for the majority of the population, personnel of other agencies are not called upon during the first home visit. Thus, therapeutic intervention in crisis situations is fairly limited. Finally, short-term placement facilities for children during crises are sorely lacking. In a picturesque statement before the Senate's Subcommittee on Children and Youth, C. Henry Kempe vividly described the problem:

> There isn't in this country a place to put a child at no notice at once with no red tape. It is easier to park a car in Denver at any time than to park a baby at 2 o'clock in the morning Saturday night. In the Middle Ages every convent had a place where somebody could place a baby, pull the bell and run like the devil and somebody would take care of that child. This is not true in our society. Today these people are very isolated. There are no neighbors to take the child if you have a big family battle going on. The child must be out of the home during a crisis. We, therefore, feel that every community should think about a safe place for a baby at moments of crisis.[1]

Fourth, since it is an important objective, achieving balance between deterrent and therapeutic approaches was mentioned above. Although an assessment of the status of current practices in this respect would require a special study, some inferences can be pieced together from the survey findings, information obtained through the literature and through unstructured in-depth studies of selected programs. Therapy-oriented professionals often mentioned that the deterrence and coercion of the law is necessary, but preferred that law enforcement should be kept as a threat to motivate conformity to the therapeutic courses prescribed. From the viewpoint of many law enforcement officers and judges, however, a report made to the police sets into motion steps prescribed by laws and regulations they are bound to uphold—investigation, evidence gathering, removal of children when necessary, and court petitions (including criminal prosecution), if warranted. The position of some judges is that, if they allowed law enforcement processes to become therapeutic instruments they would violate their own oaths. Others have found enough flexibility in their discretionary authority to work, with caseworkers and other therapists, toward shared and joint decisions or close coordination in the management of cases. The latter patterns, however, are definitely in the minority. These statements are not intended to imply that punitive approaches are necessarily characteristic of all cases reported to and investigated by the police. It would be useful to have specific information on the fate of those entering child maltreatment programs through law-enforcement channels, as compared with those entering them through therapeutically oriented services. The dichotomy was frequently mentioned in interviews, and it is prevalent in the literature. In conclusion, conflicts between therapeutic and punitive approaches remain problematic, and their effects continue to be pervasive.

Fifth, indications are that, in a sizable proportion of cases, children are left in homes where they continue to be subjected to maltreatment while child protection workers attempt to counsel the parents. Many of the children who had to be taken to hospitals or who were reported to the police were already known to protective services. Furthermore, respondents from child protective services serving two-thirds of the population acknowledged that abuse and neglect continued in varying proportions of the cases after they had become part of the active caseloads of these agencies. Four factors contributing to this situation emerge from this and other studies: inadequacies in the staffing of protective services, which limit necessary surveillance;

emphasis by caseworkers on rehabilitating parents, and on the need to gain their confidence and cooperation—at times jeopardizing the children's immediate safety; inadequacies in the legal training of caseworkers, limiting their effectiveness in court proceedings; and limitation in accessibility to trained legal counsel, which works to the same end.

Few problems were as consistently stressed by respondents from the various agencies as the problem of placement facilities, their availability and their quality. By 1972, 4.4 percent of maltreated children were still being placed in detention homes; such placement was reported in jurisdictions comprising 22.6 percent of the population. Although no data were collected in this survey about the stability of placement, evidence from sources cited earlier indicate frequent changes over short periods of time, even for children as young as 1, 2, and 3 years of age.

Sixth, assessments of the appropriateness and effectiveness of services provided to victims of maltreatment would require specific evaluations of the children beyond the scope of this work. Still, responses in the survey indicate that medical care, placement, and counseling constitute the services most generally extended to children. Because of the lack of systematic review, children are often left for long periods in foster homes and other placement facilities, with little or no further service attention. Furthermore, an overwhelming proportion of the population (84.8 percent) resided in areas where, according to respondents from child protective services, necessary services were unavailable or difficult to obtain. In this respect, responses from other agencies were not much more reassuring.

The situation concerning services to parents and families parallels that of services to children. Counseling, financial assistance, and homemaker services are the most common. Ironically, these three types of service were also among those most frequently mentioned as impossible or difficult to obtain. This means that they are well utilized where available, and acutely missed in areas where they are lacking. Vocational services are not utilized as much as might be expected from the literature linking abuse and neglect to crises emanating from employment problems. Furthermore, although most agencies frequently refer parents and guardians to mental health services, respondents' evaluations of the effectiveness of these services were less than enthusiastic. In fact, 45.8 percent of the weighted responses of public health departments were that these services were of little or no help. The reluctance of parents and guardians to seek mental health services was also widely reported in this survey. Finally, one of the most needed but weakest links in the layout of services for maltreated children and their families is long-term supportive services. Whether because of the personalities involved, family organization or disorganization, or the impinging social forces, some families require long-term or continued services to prevent the occurrence or repetition of child maltreatment.

Articulating the parts in such complex programs as those addressed to child maltreatment is as important as managing each part. Such articulation becomes more difficult when several different agencies are involved. A case in point is the discrepancy between efforts toward enhanced identification and reporting and agency capability to cope with the upsurge in reporting. Appropriate planning would have anticipated, with increases in the volume of reports, the need to expand investigation and service. The findings of this survey show that this did not occur. For example, the rates of reporting were positively associated with the caseloads of personnel in child protective agencies ($r = .48$), indicating that the rise in case identification was not matched by an equal expansion in the staffing of these services. Residual or unmet demand for services has been one of the strong arguments for persuading political decision-makers to increase agency resources, and this argument has served some agencies well. The problem revealed in the survey, however, arose from myopic approaches that emphasized reporting without giving equal weight to the emergent needs for services. For children and parents and for the providers of services the human cost of such imbalance is high.[2]

Seventh, attendance at conferences and workshops on problems of abuse and neglect was fairly prevalent. Attendance within the year prior to interviews was highest for personnel from protective agencies and lowest for hospital medical personnel. In many of the agencies training programs were mainly attended by heads of departments or supervisors. The effectiveness of training activities cannot be evaluated solely on the basis of attendance at meetings and workshops, however; it is also necessary to consider the quality of information available at these meetings, which in this field remains at a low level.

Eighth, the open and diffuse definitions and criteria for child maltreatment invite unsystematic collection of evidence. These factors also introduce subjectivity in the selection and evaluation of evidence, as well as in the exercise of judgment in reaching decisions. Individual caseworkers and law enforcement officers often make decisions that may entail serious consequences: to investigate reports; to leave the children in the custody of potentially or actually abusive or neglectful parents and guardians; to remove the children and change custody; to place children removed from their homes; to provide or arrange for services for children and parents; to reunite families; to extend or to terminate follow-up services; and to terminate parental custody and free the children for adoption. Information obtained through this study indicates that there are no consistent rules for decision making in connection with these problems. Instead, they vary according to agencies, according to professional backgrounds, and quite frequently according to individuals. The variability of decisions inevitably raises questions about their validity and equity.

Ninth, data on program coordination show that only 15.6 percent of the population resided in areas where interagency collaboration had been worked out at the case-management level. An additional 28.8 percent were in areas where interagency liaisons were still at the administrative level, with meetings attended mainly by heads of agencies or their representatives. In contrast to actual case management, the purpose of administrative relations is to clarify the roles and responsibilities of the respective agencies. Finally, 55.6 percent of the population lived in communities where neither level of coordination existed. Among the problems most frequently mentioned by respondents was the lack of interagency cooperation and the non-centralized handling of reports and investigations.

It is interesting to note that the prevalence of perceived interagency problems in case management was related to the level of coordination in a curvilinear manner. Respondents from communities where no liaisons existed and from those where close case-management coordination was reported were less likely to report interagency problems than respondents from agencies characterized by administrative forms of coordination. The three levels of coordination seem to represent evolutionary phases in the process of building interagency linkages. In the first phase, with no coordination, awareness is likely to be low; consequently, agencies see no challenge to their roles and routines. Attempts toward administrative coordination in the second phase imply a growing awareness. This change signals a challenge to the established reciprocal roles and responsibilities of

TABLE 5.1
GENERAL ASSESSMENT OF AGENCY EFFECTIVENESS

Agencies and Assessment	Organizations and Responses						
	CPS	PHS	SCH	HMD	HSS	CRT	POL
All agencies in the area							
Very effective	25.6	15.1	23.2	28.1	23.8	35.0	44.3
Somewhat effective	62.5	72.4	56.6	42.1	49.8	57.8	44.6
Not very effective	9.1	10.9	13.0	15.0	16.6	0.8	9.3
Not effective at all	1.7	0.1	3.7	2.4	1.7	2.7	1.0
Don't know	1.1	1.5	3.6	12.4	8.1	3.7	0.7
Respondent's own agency							
Very effective	39.1	18.7	23.9	41.9	40.1	44.8	62.0
Somewhat effective	58.3	66.5	57.0	37.9	45.9	50.4	28.9
Not very effective	2.5	9.7	14.3	12.4	9.9	1.7	5.4
Not effective at all	....	3.9	1.8	2.2	1.1	1.2	1.7
Don't know	....	1.3	3.0	5.7	3.0	1.9	1.9

the agencies, heightening the perception of problems in interagency relations. The third phase, in which new routines have developed around closer case-management coordination, tends to resolve some of the problems characteristic of the second phase.

Finally, it would be only appropriate in this summary assessment to indicate the respondents' overall appraisals of the effectiveness of the various agencies in their area, as well as of their respective agencies, in dealing with child abuse and neglect. Table 5.1 presents the results of these appraisals, which exhibit a lack of conviction about overall program effectiveness. In varying measures, respondents tended to attribute greater effectiveness to their own agencies than to others in their communities. Since responses designating the agencies as "very effective" represent the clearest positive evaluations, the proportions of respondents who gave these answers were tabulated in

TABLE 5.2
FORMS OF COORDINATION AND PERCENTAGES OF
"VERY EFFECTIVE" ASSESSMENTS

Forms of Coordination	Organizations and Responses						
	CPS	PHN	SCH	HMD	HSS	CRT	POL
Case-Management level	23.2	22.2	28.0	19.5	27.4	34.6	48.6
Administrative coordination	24.7	9.7	24.5	12.1	16.4	19.3	25.6
No coordination	26.8	15.8	21.0	38.0	27.7	42.2	52.8

relation to the levels of coordination in their areas. The distributions (Table 5.2) corroborate the conclusions reached earlier concerning the three phases in the development of interagency working relations. With minor exceptions, agencies in communities with coordination at the case-management level and those with no coordination at all were most likely to view as very effective overall agency performance in dealing with abuse and neglect.

ENHANCING PERFORMANCE

As with other complex and multidimensional programs, recommendations toward enhanced coping with child maltreatment may be viewed at two levels—the specific components of programs and the larger picture of relations among the components. While the first eight of the nine goals outlined earlier can be generally considered to address specific components and aspects, the ninth concerns the broader question of coordination. No attempt will be made to present the following comments in a point-by-point correspondence to the goals, for individual recommendations are not necessarily coterminous with individual goals. Finally, it should be mentioned that the points to be made are neither new nor unfamiliar to readers knowledgeable in the field. Nevertheless, because child maltreatment is a problem of such scope and seriousness, their continued articulation—even at the risk of repetition—is necessary.

Specific Program Components

The contrast between summary assessments of the current status of programs and the goals and functions of those programs makes readily apparent a number of directions for program development. To begin with, primary prevention of child maltreatment will require public education, not only in identification and reporting, but also in the substantive aspects of parenting, child care, and the rights of children and parents. School curricula, civic organizations, and the mass media constitute important channels for such programs. Admittedly, education is a slow process, but its results are enduring. Primary prevention will also require sustained efforts to find ways to identify risk populations for whom special educational and service programs can be specifically tailored. It should be noted that program components addressed to primary prevention will remain weak as long as epidemiological knowledge remains underdeveloped.

Well-reasoned options and guidelines for legislation on the reporting of child abuse and neglect have been prepared.[3] Also, many communities have experimented with ways of improving identification and reporting, and pockets of reluctance or indifference have become better recognized. In addition to statutory change to remove legal liability for unconfirmable reports and to mandate reporting on the part of certain professions and agencies, combining mass-media campaigns, the provision of special telephone lines, and continuous coverage at all hours has proven effective in susbstantially increasing the rates of reporting. Since rates of confirmation decrease as rates of reporting rise, special attention must be directed to initial investigations and to the management of registeries.

No information is available concerning the impact of an investigation upon families that were falsely reported. Such investigations could be harassing, however, and cause "labeling" among friends and neighbors, as well as in records—with unhealthy consequences for both parent-child relations and for the family as a whole. On the other hand, complacent reactions to reports because of an increased probability of nonconfirmation would render useless identification and reporting efforts. Therefore, attempts to increase reporting should be coupled with efforts to enhance accuracy in reporting. Stationing protective service personnel in schools and orienting school health examinations toward screening for abuse and neglect are examples of means toward these dual objectives.

Increased reporting should never be seen as an end in itself, but only as a step toward the delivery of appropriate services. Shortages in resources, staffing, and services are acute, especially in communities where reporting has been rising rapidly. Evidence so far seems to demonstrate that it is far easier to increase identification and reporting than to accommodate the children and parents identified. It should be possible to make fairly reliable estimates of necessary expansion on the basis of experience in communities with high rates of reporting. Such estimates could be used to anticipate needs in communities about to embark on efforts toward increased identification and reporting. Alan Sussman and Stephan J. Cohen, offering guidelines for legislation, underscore the danger of a disjunction between reporting and services. "Mere reporting," they point out, "without concern for the treatment of the child or the problems which caused the harm, may be meaningless if not harmful. For this reason, the purpose of this Act is described as the promotion of reporting in *a manner* which will foster the provision of necessary protective services."[4]

Lists of the types of services lacking in the various communities have been presented and discussed at other points in this report. Emphasis should be placed, however, on placement facilities and services. The utility and feasibility of crisis intervention facilities oriented to short-term placement and crisis resolution have been already demonstrated.[5] Early response to diffuse crisis situations is second in importance only to effective primary prevention. Long-term or continued supportive services need to be developed for families whose conditions call for such services. Long-term placement also requires special attention, not only to availability, but also to quality. To avoid leaving children in "limbo" for long periods of time in foster homes, protective agencies should institute periodic reviews of cases at regular intervals, in which members of the staff other than the caseworker in charge would take part.

The heavy reliance upon foster homes also calls for serious consideration to the development of standards, investigations, and licensure in this area. In addition to services required for separated children, protective service workers will need to develop options to regulate parents' rights to visit so that they do not become stressful to foster parents and to the children. They also need to develop criteria for determining when permanent separation from parents should be sought, to free children for adoption. A periodic review of cases should help time such decisions more appropriately for the children's best interest. In order to address these matters more effectively, most protective services need to become better acquainted with the laws and to have greater accessibility to specialized legal assistance.

Because of the present openness of criteria defining the basis for decisions vital to children and parents, and the likelihood that this openness will continue in the foreseeable future, it would be advisable to consider developing decision making patterns that would avoid individual, subjective influences. As mentioned earlier, one approach to this problem is to limit individual decisions in favor of those made by two or more persons. These persons could be from the same agency or better yet from different agencies; similarly, they could either have the same professional background or could represent different professions. Although such group decision-making is characteristic of therapeutic teams within certain settings, it is much less prevalent in interagency functioning. Special training is needed to establish a structure and tradition of joint decisions involving personnel from different agencies and professional backgrounds. It is through such decision-making structures and traditions that many of the dilemmas and value conflicts discussed in the second chapter of this report can be resolved. This would require coordination among agencies at the level of case management.

It was not our intention in the foregoing discussion to become involved either in the details of the specific components of programs on child maltreatment, or in the particulars of approaches to investigations or service modalities. Rather, the purpose was to emphasize a few salient points that have pervasive effects upon the performance of total programs. We turn now to the larger picture of program coordination.

Coordination at the Community Level

Specialization is an inevitable outcome of differences in the nature of problems to which services and other forms of intervention are addressed. Specialization also results from the growth of knowledge about these problems and from the corresponding technological developments. In many respects, however, functional specialization has resulted in considerable proliferation and fragmentation in the structure and actual delivery of services. This situation is further complicated by the involvement of various jurisdictional levels (federal, state, and local) in public programs. Adding to this complexity is the influence of incrementalism in program development.

One factor contributing to piecemeal additions and reforms in human services involves ambiguities and shifts in emphasis between two types of programs that, for lack of better terms, will be referred to as *functional* and *categorical*. Functional programs are problem oriented, regardless of the populations that encounter the problem. Thus, health care is oriented to pathology and injuries, no matter who experiences them—abused children, other children, or adults requiring care. In contrast, categorical programs are organized around the needs of certain categories of the population, such as the aged, children, veterans, and so on. One underlying factor in the many generations of reorganization of human services at the various levels of government, especially in the Department of Health, Education, and Welfare, has been vacillation between functional and categorical program arrangements. Similar problems characterize attempts to organize programs on child abuse and neglect in many communities, where functionally oriented agencies are attempting to take on the categorical responsibilities of coordination. Thus, in addition to providing the functional services in which they specialize, hospitals and mental health clinics are becoming involved in coordinating the activities of other agencies. In fact, some arrangements seem to duplicate already existing programs on child maltreatment in certain communities.

It is important to recognize that both components need to be considered in the proposed model for the structure and delivery of services concerning child maltreatment. Involved children and parents share with other sectors of society many problems that fall within the domains of the same functional agencies. The similarity of these needs makes it equally important that program development be done with one eye on the nature of the problem and related service requirements, and the other on the broader context of services. To avoid duplication and unnecessary overlap, programs organized around problems of abuse and neglect should build upon existing functional services, where they can serve common needs. For example, an important function is served by designating and advertising a special telephone number to call for reports or help on problems of abuse and neglect. However, confusion must arise when the public is bombarded by special numbers for each type of crisis, such as numbers to call for suicide prevention, for help with drug addiction, venereal diseases, or unwanted pregnancies, for poison control, and for squad ambulances, to name only a few. A contextual view would lead to the consolidation of emergency situations into one easy number that people can memorize. It then becomes the responsibility of recipients of the calls, who are in states of mind more conducive to distinguishing among the types of emergencies, to make the appropriate arrangements. Finally, certain problems, and therefore certain specialized needs, may arise in dealing with child maltreatment, as is the case with crisis intervention or foster home placement.

A partial list of functional program services and activities would include: medical screening; treatment; restorative care; mental health services; counseling to children, parents, and foster parents; nutritional services; emergency placement; temporary placement; adoption services; day-care facilities; education; legal representation; vocational services (training, rehabilitation, and placement); income maintenance and support; family housing; and homemaker services. Many of these headings include a variety of types administered by various agencies. For example, there are programs such as those associated with unemployment insurance, veterans' benefits, social security, disability and other benefits, aid to dependent children, and other income-maintenance services. Some of these are more applicable to children, others to parents, and still others to whole families. With the exception of the type of crisis intervention needed in child maltreatment cases, and possibly with the exception of placement services, the rest of these are oriented to problems common to other children and adults. There should be no need to duplicate any of these services within a hospital, a protective agency, a center, or other newly created entities. Rather, efforts toward building a community program to deal with child maltreatment should be directed to improving and expanding available services, if needed, and to developing nonexistent ones.

The coordination of these services and activities calls for the other

FIGURE 5.1

A DIAGRAMMATIC SCHEME FOR PROGRAM STRUCTURE

Functional Programs	Categorical-Coordinative Programs		
	Child Maltreatment	The Disabled	Multiproblem Aged
Health Care	— — —	— — — — — —	— — — — — —	— — —
Restorative Care	— — —	— — — — — —	— — — — — —	— — —
Mental Health Services	— — —	— — — — — —	— — — — — —	— — —
Psychological Counseling	— — —	— — — — — —	— — — — — —	— — —
Nutritional Services	— — —	— — — — — —	— — — — — —	— — —
Crisis Intervention	— — —	— — — — — —	— — — — — —	— — —
Long-Term Placement	— — —	— — — — — —	— — — — — —	— — —
Emergency Placement	— — —	— — —		
Adoption Services	— — —	— — —		
Day-Care Facilities	— — —	— — —		
Education	— — —	— — — — —	— — — — —	— — —
Legal Representation	— — —	— — — — —	— — — — —	— — —
Vocational and Employment Services	— — —	— — — — — —	— — —	
Income Maintenance	— — —	— — — — —	— — — — —	— — —
Housing	— — —	— — — — —	— — — — —	— — —
Homemaker Services	— — —	— — — — —	— — — — —	— — —
Institutional Care	— — —	— — — — —	— — — — —	— — —

component of the programs—the categorically oriented agencies. The relations between the two types (functional and categorical) are represented graphically in Figure 5.1. Categorical-coordinative agencies are needed for those sectors of the population with multiple problems whose needs fall within the domains of large numbers of agencies. The disabled, the aged, and multiproblem families, including those involved in abuse and neglect, constitute examples of such sectors. Focusing now on child maltreatment, responsibilities of the categorical-coordinative agencies would include:

Activities related to case identification, such as maintaining telephones for that purpose; continuous coverage of these phones and other means of reporting; mounting campaigns for early identification and reporting; and building liaisons with schools, day-care centers, and other institutions where case identification could be improved.

Investigating reports or participating with law enforcement officers in their investigations.

Keeping centralized records on reports and active cases; such records should be oriented to case management, reflecting an up-to-date picture of the pathways of children and parents through the system, of the services they have received, of decisions in their cases, and of their current status.

Case management through functional agencies providing services and benefits, as well as through the legal aspects of the situation.

Arranging for periodical review of cases and for joint assessments and decisions at important points in the process.

Assessment and development of the community resources and services needed by children and families involved in the problem.

Arranging for public and professional education programs on the prevention of and therapy for child maltreatment.

If the categorical-coordinative agencies are to perform these functions effectively, they must have legal mandates rendering the practices of other public agencies consistent with these responsibilities. Thus, the coordinative agency should be notified as soon as reports of suspected child maltreatment are received by other agencies. The participation of coordinative agency personnel in initial investigations should also be required by law.

In addition to structuring legally the interrelations between the functionally oriented and the categorical-coordinative agencies, the latter should be given the resources to contract for services their clients need. This could be done through the direct purchase of services from such sources as hospitals and clinics, and from private vendors. Another possibility would be to extend resources to another public agency so that it could improve its own staffing, and thus accommodate the needs of abused and neglected children and their families. An example of the latter arrangement would be providing funds so that local health departments could establish positions for public health nurses whose time would be devoted to these problems.

It should be noted that the role of categorical-coordinative agencies as defined here does not include involvement in therapy, placement, or other services around which functional programs are organized. Focusing the categorical-coordinative agencies' role on case management should help resolve a number of the dilemmas and conflicts mentioned at the onset of this report. No longer should coordinative

personnel feel they need to gain the confidence of parents for therapeutic purposes, risking the safety of children, at times, in order to do
so. Counseling and therapeutic intervention, in this arrangement,
become the responsibility of others. By the same token, separating responsibilities for placement would also limit the potential for role
conflicts. Finally, these agencies' noninvolvement in the direct provision of services that fall within the domains of functional programs
should both reduce the potential for interorganizational conflicts and
eliminate unnecessary duplication of effort.

The most likely candidates for the categorical-coordinative role are
the child protective services. However, their responsibilities and,
more important, their present practices would need to undergo major
change if they were to enact this role as defined above. While special-
izing in the seven functions comprising this role, they would no
longer be directly responsible for the placement of children, nor
would they engage in psychological and other intensive counseling of
children, parents, or foster parents. Instead, the counseling role of
personnel in these agencies would be limited to providing information necessary for referrals and other aspects of case management. It
should be noted, however, that the division of labor described in this
model does not negate the utility of multiprofessional teams within
given therapeutic settings, such as in hospitals, or multiagency committees operating on a community-wide basis to assess progress and
render decisions on cases. The latter could be organized either on a
regular basis to deal with all cases, or in an *ad hoc* fashion for cases
with particular characteristics and needs.

The Fundamental Issues

However visible child maltreatment has become as a national
issue, it basically represents symptoms of more fundamental problems besetting the institution of the family. Although treating the
symptoms is an important objective in itself, greater attention must
be directed to preventive measures. Political wisdom would call for
capitalizing on the current public attention given child maltreatment
to introduce measures addressing underlying problems. The diffuseness, complexity, and pervasiveness of these problems make
them more difficult to articulate in a way that catches the public's
awareness and mobilizes its support.

The family as an institution has steadily grown more fragile. The prevalent nuclear type enjoys less of the social and economic security afforded in traditional intergenerational families. Interaction among the limited number of members is more intensive and provides fewer alternatives at times of conflict and tension. In a largely wage-earning society, changes in the economic picture and in the labor market exert considerable influence upon the family. Sickness, illness, disability, aging, unemployment, and other forms of dependency add to the burdens of this frail institution. Careerism, the need for multiple sources of income to cope with rising living costs, and the new inclination toward freedom (meaning concern with personal individualistic interests) have further weakened the family structure. Some public social welfare measures have even contributed toward the same results. In summary, the family has become the collecting point for the effects of stresses and strains in almost all other institutions. These stresses and strains are neither bound to given socioeconomic strata, nor to a particular ethnic or geographic distribution. Furthermore, certain families have become so marginal or troubled that their needs for supportive services are of long-term or indefinite duration.

It is neither possible nor necessarily desirable to attempt to turn back the clock on institutional change. Rather, the objective should be to provide the necessary public mechanisms that would assist families in need in coping with the impact of such change. The human consequences of the failure of the family become clearly evident when one considers the significance of the societal functions served by this institution and the fact that no alternative institutional forms have been evolved. It is the locus for the transmission of society's norms and values and for the nurturance of a variety of other human needs, as well as the source of the most basic forms of security. Certainly human services in one way or another contribute to the resolution of problems touching the family. In most cases, however, these services are organized around and provided to individuals who happen to be members of families. Most services, moreover, are oriented to specific types of pathologies or problems, and families marginal in most dimensions find it difficult to qualify for such services. Unlike other institutions, such as medicine, law, the economy, or politics, there are no public mechanisms for the support of the family as a unit when problems arise. Nowhere does the need for such a mechanism become clearer than in relation to the prevention and control of abuse and neglect of children and other family members. In this respect I recommend:

1. The development of community family centers, possibly designated as Family Maintenance Organizations (FMOs). These would provide the categorical programs for vulnerable children and families.

2. That a campaign of public education be launched on symptoms of family problems, and that families be urged to avail themselves of preventive services through these FMOs: models for such campaigns are fairly numerous in the field of public health.

3. That these organizations do not become centers for divorce, abortion, or marriage, but rather mobilization centers for available and needed services and resources to bear upon the problems of client families; these functions have already been specified in the previous section.

The Role of the Federal Government

The fragmentation, duplication, gaps, overlaps, and generally poor coordination characteristic of community-level programs on child maltreatment are matched by those at the federal level. For example, the newly established Center on Child Abuse Prevention and Treatment, which administers the 1974 Act and related demonstrations, is part of the Children's Bureau and the Office of Child Development. Federal responsibilities for protective services, however, are located in the Social and Rehabilitation Services Administration. And, while the operational aspects of protective services are at the SRS, related research and technical personnel are in the Children's Bureau. In addition, two national centers with overlapping domains (National Center for Child Advocacy and National Center on Child Abuse Prevention and Treatment) coexist within the Children's Bureau. The problem is compounded by unresolved ambiguities and by conflicts about the roles of federal, regional, and state levels of government. However responsibilities may eventually be distributed among these levels—that is, wherever the authority for change may ultimately lie, several issues warrant serious consideration.

The first involves the consolidation of program elements at higher levels of government and the clear articulation of the relations among these elements. There are no defensible reasons why demonstrations, research, and technical capabilities should be located in one agency and the operational arm of protective services in another. A consolidation of these segments into one agency would be advantageous from both administrative and program viewpoints. The following also need further clarification and coordination of their roles and functions at higher levels of government: the National Center on Child Abuse and Neglect, the National Center for Child Advocacy, such other welfare services as adoption and foster home placement, and day-care and other family services.

The second issue concerns resources. The picture revealed in this survey raises a general question about the extent of public commitment to preventing child maltreatment and alleviating the suffering it causes. As has been pointed out earlier, support to child protective services has remained relatively low, and the rapid increase in case identification and reporting in many communities has created serious problems in the delivery of services, since capacities have not kept pace with demands. Because needed resources cannot be provided locally, this problem requires attention at the higher levels of government.

The third recommendation is for the development of long-range perspectives on the problem of child maltreatment and on related programs and resources as well. Most of the funds made available through the 1974 Act and through resources pooled by several HEW agencies prior to the Act were invested in various types of demonstration programs throughout the country. In the preoccupation with the enactment and implementation of laws, however, some fundamental questions have not been answered. Important among these is the question of the purpose of it all, which can be answered only by looking beyond the current generation of demonstration programs. Are the long-range considerations to demonstrate that effective programs can be mounted, with the idea that appropriations might be increased to generalize them to other parts of the country? or to demonstrate the methods and results of mounting effective programs in certain communities, with the hope that other communities would emulate them, using resources of their own? or are the demonstrations ends in themselves? In order to maximize the yield from demonstrations of this type, long-range perspectives must be developed early in the planning and implementation process.

Traditionally, the role of the higher levels of government has included developing and maintaining standards, evolving technical capabilities to guide local programs, conducting research and demonstrations, and disseminating the results. Although, in line with the current national mood, reduction in the size of government has become a popular cause, it would be a mistake to limit agency staffing in an indiscriminate manner. The waste that results from a shortage of qualified technicians can far exceed the savings realized. Furthermore, the various communities look to state, regional, and federal agencies for standards and guidance on problems connected with services and program organization.

Important also is the diffusion of new ideas and approaches—diffusion here referring to both providing information on innovations and to their implementation or adoption. Diffusion thus means systematically and purposefully encouraging the adoption of the new ideas, techniques, or organizational patterns. In most instances, however, this process has been limited to publishing and distributing material on the results of research and demonstrations. Efforts may go one step farther to include presentations in conferences, workshops, or other gatherings. At best, these approaches can make participants aware of new findings. Nevertheless, knowledge in itself is not sufficient for change. If agency personnel are to be motivated to adopt innovations they must have knowledge not only about an innovation, but also about the ways it relates to their own programs and what its adoption would mean in terms of established routines, the structure of roles and responsibilities, and the demand for and availability of resources.

These issues require careful, expert, and intensive analyses of the situations of the agencies in question. Unless such a serious effort toward the diffusion of innovations is undertaken, the results of research and demonstrations conducted at high cost will remain largely academic. We recommend that a pilot study be organized around this approach to diffusion, dealing with a limited number of innovations and a small number of communities. If effective, the study should be expanded, especially if one of the primary objectives of demonstrations is to encourage communities throughout the country to emulate the successful models that emerge.

Finally, a note on evaluation seems appropriate. Deviations from ideals in human services are common; they vary in frequency and intensity from one program to another, and from one sector of the population to another. The ideals, however, serve the important functions of setting goals and providing standards against which deviations can be identified and assessed. These deviations give rise to the search for remedies and to the identification of alternative policies and plans. Given the complexity of factors and outcomes involved in social policies and programs, it can be assumed that most planning has a balance of positive and negative effects. Policy and program decisions are often made, however, without the full realization of their secondary effects. As inadequacies and negative effects of earlier actions become apparent, new decisions and actions become necessary. Harold Lasswell sees the essential role of systematic data gathering in this continual process of policy and program planning, which includes

> the intelligence function, i.e., the gathering of information which may include either information which suggests a problem for policymakers' attention or information for the formulation of alternatives. A second function is the recommendation of one or more possible policy alternatives. A third is the prescription or enactment of one among several proposed alternative solutions. A fourth is the invocation of the adopted alternative, and a fifth is its application in specific situations by executive or enforcement offices. A sixth stage of the decision process is the appraisal of the effectiveness of the prescribed alternative, and the seventh is the termination of the original policy.[6]

Concern with policy and program analysis has given rise to evaluative research. Much has been written on methodological approaches to evaluation, the roles of evaluators, and the contexts of evaluation.[7] Nevertheless, pressures of time, inappropriate patterns of funding, and defensive attitudes on the part of those in charge of agency affairs have combined to produce evaluations that are conceptually limited and methodologically faulty. Well-designed and meaningful evaluations are costly and threatening.

Emphasis in reported studies has been placed primarily on validity in measures of outcome, that is, change in clients and their conditions consistent with program objectives. Equal attention needs to be given to methods of assessing equity and organizational responsiveness in regard to both processes and outcomes. This calls for the inclusion of information on the opinions of clients and other segments of the public in data systems used in policy and program planning. The opinions of personnel engaged in the provision of services and law enforcement also constitute an important input for evaluation. These opinions will need to be elicited in independent surveys, rather than through the official agency channels. Furthermore, because public policies and programs are often national in scope, cross-national comparisons become an important source of alternatives. Four types of data, then, are necessary for sound policy and program analysis: information obtained directly from applicants, clients, and related segments of the public; information (based on their own opinions) from providers of services, investigators of reports and administrators in these programs; official agency reports; and comparative information on similar agencies and programs in other societies, especially those with comparable socioeconomic conditions.

Furthermore, it should be noted that one-shot evaluations are not as useful as long-term programs of research and monitoring. Physicians and weather forecasters have learned that a change in readings is more significant for prognosis and prediction than an initial set of measures. It is also important that longitudinal monitoring systems not be focused exclusively on outcome, but include explanatory information as well. Emphasis in the selection of explanatory factors should be on controllable variables, so that they would not only suggest directions for change, but also make such change possible.

 NOTES

1. BACKGROUND AND SCOPE: PROBLEM AND APPROACHES

1. See Vincent DeFrancis, *The Fundamentals of Child Protection* (Denver: The American Humane Association, 1955).

2. Theodore Solomon, "History and Demography of Child Abuse," *Pediatrics*, Vol. 51, No. 4, Part II (1973), p. 774.

3. Mason P. Thomas, Jr., "Child Abuse and Neglect, Part I: Historical Overview, Legal Matrix, and Social Perspectives," *North Carolina Law Review*, Vol. 50 (February 1972), p. 305.

4. Act of April 9, 1912, ch. 73, 37 Stat. 79.

5. 42 U.S.C.A. §§ 620–26 (1974) [SS Act Title IV B].

6. See for example Marilyn Heins, "From Us—Doctors' View of Child Abuse," *Canadian Welfare*, Vol. 50, No. 5 (1974); M. E. Alberts, "Child Abuse," *Journal of the Iowa Medical Society*, Vol. 62 (May 1972); Sanford N. Katz, *When Parents Fail: The Law's Response to Family Breakdown* (Boston: Beacon Press, 1972); Monrad G. Paulsen, "The Legal Framework of Child Protection," *Columbia Law Review*, Vol. 66 (April 1966); Shirley L. Bean, "The Parents' Center Project: A Multiservice Approach to the Prevention of Child Abuse," *Child Welfare*, Vol. 50, No. 5 (1971); Joseph Goldstein, Anna Freud, and Albert J. Solnit, *Beyond the Best Interests of the Child* (New York: The Free Press, 1973); David G. Gil, *Violence Against Children* (Cambridge, Mass.: Harvard University Press, 1970).

7. Thomas, "Child Abuse and Neglect, Part I," pp. 293–349.

8. Jean Nazarro, "Child Abuse and Neglect," *Exceptional Children*, Vol. 40, No. 5 (1974), p. 353.

9. DeFrancis, *The Fundamentals of Child Protection*.

10. Alan Sussman and Stephan J. Cohen, *Reporting Child Abuse and Neglect: Guidelines for Legislation* (Cambridge, Mass.: Ballinger Publishing Company, 1975), p. 125.

11. See Thomas, "Child Abuse and Neglect, Part I," pp. 293–349.

12. Nazarro, "Child Abuse and Neglect," p. 253.

13. 42 U.S.C.A. §§ 5101–6 (1975 Cur. Supp.) [Child Abuse Prevention and Treatment Act].

14. 42 U.S.C.A. §§ 1397f. (Feb. 1975 Cur. Supp.) [SS Act Title XX].

15. See Vincent DeFrancis and Carroll L. Lucht, *Child Abuse Legislation in the 1970's* (Denver: American Humane Association, 1974).

16. See Marvin R. Burt and Louis H. Blair, *Options for Improving the Care of Neglected and Dependent Children* (Washington, D.C.: The Urban Institute, 1971); Marilyn Heins, "Child Abuse—Analysis of a Current Epidemic," *Michigan Medicine,* Vol. 68 (September 1969), pp. 887–91; Ray E. Helfer, *Child Abuse and Neglect: The Diagnostic Process and Treatment Programs* (Washington, D.C.: Office of Child Development, 1975); David G. Gil, "Unraveling Child Abuse," *American Journal of Orthopsychiatry,* Vol. 45, No. 3 (1975), p. 346; Harris D. Riley, "The Battered Child Syndrome: General and Medical Aspects," *Southern Medical Journal,* Vol. 58, No. 3 (1970), pp. 9–13.

17. Sampling for the earlier survey was devised by the University of Michigan's Survey Research Center. For a detailed description of their approaches to population sampling see Leslie Kish and Irene Hess, *The Survey Research Center's National Sample of Dwellings* (Ann Arbor: Institute for Social Research, The University of Michigan, 1965).

2. Contextual Issues, Conflicts, and Dilemmas

1. Three approaches suggest themselves in creating categories out of continua such as those represented by the sample scores on the seven indices (Rights of Parents and Children, State intervention, Decision Criteria, Effectiveness of Technology, Punitive Versus Therapeutic Orientation, Conflicts Between Punitive and Therapeutic Approaches, and Role Conflict). The problem is one of selecting appropriate points for defining the categories. One way to establish these points is to divide the scale into equal intervals. Another way is to divide the sample into equal groups regardless of the points on the scale that define these groupings. While the first approach creates equal scale intervals, the second results in equal categories of people; both represent arbitrarily created classes. A third approach was used in this analysis. Histograms representing the distributions of sample scores were examined in order to identify forms of clustering and therefore determine the natural points of differentiation among categories. The objective was to arrive at conceptually more meaningful classifications by "carving at the joints," to use Abraham Kaplan's metaphor, as it appears in his *Conduct of Inquiry: Methodology for Behavioral Science* (San Francisco: Chandler Publishing Company, 1964), p. 50.

2. Thomas Hobbes, *Leviathan,* Molesworth Edition, Vol. 3 (London: J. Bohn, 1839–45), p. 257.

3. *Ibid.,* p. 188.

4. Walter I. Trattner, *From Poor Law to Welfare State: A History of Social Welfare in America* (New York: The Free Press, 1974), p. 23.

5. C. J. Flammang, *The Police and the Underprotected Child* (Springfield, Ill.: Charles C. Thomas Publishers, 1970), p. 15.

6. *Ibid.*

7. Sanford N. Katz, *When Parents Fail: The Law's Response to Family Breakdown* (Boston: Beacon Press, 1971), p. 5.

8. H. H. Foster, Jr. and D. J. Freed, "A Bill of Rights for Children," *Family Law Quarterly,* Vol. 6 (Winter 1972), p. 345.

9. Hillary Rodham, "Children Under the Law," *Harvard Educational Review,* Vol. 43, No. 4 (1973), p. 492.

10. Harold L. Wilensky and Charles N. Lebeaux, *Industrial Society and Social Welfare* (New York: Free Press, 1965), p. 71.

11. Andrew Jay Kleinfeld, "The Balance of Power Among Infants, Their Parents and the State, Part II," *Family Law Quarterly,* Vol. 4 (December 1970), p. 410.

12. Katz, *When Parents Fail,* p. 5.

13. *Ibid.,* pp. 3–13.

14. Alfred Kadushin, *Child Welfare Services,* 2d. ed. (New York: Macmillan Company, 1974).

15. Alan Sussman and Stephen J. Cohen, *Reporting Child Abuse and Neglect: Guidelines for Legislation* (Cambridge, Mass.: Ballinger Publishing Company, 1975), p. xxiii.

16. Report to the President: *White House Conference on Children* (Washington, D.C.: U.S. Government Printing Office, 1970).

17. *Ibid.*

18. Charles Perrow, "Hospitals: Technology, Structure and Goals" in James G. March, ed., *Handbook of Organizations* (Chicago: Rand McNally and Company, 1965), p. 912.

19. *Ibid.,* p. 926.

20. For advocates of professional casework, see Edmund A. Sherman et al., *Service to Children in Their Own Homes: Its Nature and Outcomes* (New York: Child Welfare League of America, 1973); Elizabeth Elmer, *Children in Jeopardy: A Study of Abused Minors and Their Families* (Pittsburgh: University of Pittsburgh Press, 1967). For advocates of nonprofessional help, see M. E. Alberts, "Child Abuse," *Journal of Iowa Medical Society,* Vol. 62 (May 1972), p. 242; C. Henry Kempe, "A Practical Approach to the Protection of the Abused Child and Rehabilitation of the Abusing Parent," *Pediatrics,* Vol. 51 (April 1973), pp. 804–9. For advocates of Parents Anonymous, see Coleman McCarthy, "Suffer the Little Children," *Washington Post* (March 27, 1973); H. M. Feinstein et al., "Group Therapy for Mothers with Infanticidal Impulses," *American Journal of Psychiatry,* Vol. 120 (1964), pp. 882–86.

21. C. Henry Kempe, "A Practical Approach," pp. 804–12.

22. Martin Rein, "The Social Service Crisis," *Transaction,* Vol. 1 (May 1964), pp. 3–6.

23. *Ibid.*

24. Roland L. Warren, "The Concerting of Decisions as a Variable in Organizational Interaction," in Matthew F. Tuite, Roger K. Chisholm, and Michael Radnor, eds., *Interorganizational Decision Making* (Chicago: Aldine Publishing Company, 1972), p. 22.

25. *Ibid.*

3. Magnitude of the Problem and Epidemiological Patterns

1. Alan Sussman and Stephan J. Cohen, *Reporting Child Abuse and Neglect: Guidelines for Legislation* (Cambridge, Mass.: Ballinger Publishing Company, 1975), pp. 117–18.

2. *Ibid.*, pp. 121–26.

3. *Ibid.*, pp. 125–26.

4. For a more detailed discussion, see Sussman and Cohen, *Reporting Child Abuse and Neglect*, pp. 87–96.

5. This estimate was based on statistics provided by the U.S. Department of Commerce, Bureau of the Census, *City and County Data Book: 1972* (Washington, D.C.: U.S. Government Printing Office, 1973), p. 78.

6. Norman A. Polansky, Carolyn Hally, and Nancy F. Polansky, *State of Knowledge of Child Neglect: Final Report to the Community Service Administration* (Athens: The University of Georgia, 1974).

7. Sussman and Cohen, *Reporting Child Abuse and Neglect*, p. 125.

8. Two important relationships were discovered to follow clear patterns conceptually and in the data: *a*, the rate of confirmation of abuse reports, defined as the number of confirmed abuse cases divided by the total number of reports at any level of reporting; and *b*, the identified abuse rate, defined as the number of confirmed abuse cases divided by the number of children in the population, for any level of reporting. Thus, both relationships are functions of the rate of reporting and will be referred to hereafter as $S(R)$ and $A(R)$, respectively, where R is the rate of reporting per child (in other words, the proportion of children upon whom reports are being received).

Conceptually it is clear that $A(R)$ increases monotonically throughout its entire domain, since the number of confirmed abuse cases either increases or remains the same as the rate of reporting increases. Conversely, except for extremely small reporting rates, $S(R)$ decreases monotonically, since the confirmation rate is expected to be high for moderately small reporting rates and low for higher rates. This can easily be seen in the extreme case where the entire population of children is being reported, and, clearly, only the actual cases of abuse would result in confirmed reports. For extremely small reporting rates, however, no clear conceptual pattern exists because the value $S(\Phi)$ is indeterminate.

Additionally, other patterns can be derived. First, $S(R)$ and $A(R)$ are clearly related by their definitions. In fact, $S(R) = A(R)/R$, thus making either derivable from the other. Secondly, $A(R)$ and $S(R)$ converge to the "true" rate of child abuse, that is, $S(1) = A(1) = $ "true" rate of abuse.

The objective was to identify this "true" rate of abuse by identifying a family of curves which possess all these characteristics, and from this family to choose the one best fitting the data collected in the study. Given this exact curve, the "true" rate of abuse can be estimated, as well as other relationships important to the policy-level decision process, such as the proportion of the "true" cases being identified and the rate of nonconfirmation for any level of reporting.

The following is the family of functions that has the appropriate properties:

$$\text{Let} \quad G(R) = G(R;a,b,c) = c \cdot \int_{o}^{R} t^{a-1}(1-t)^{b-1}dt,$$

where a, b, and c are parameters whose values were to be estimated from the data. Once these values were computed, the estimated "true" rate of child abuse becomes:

$$G(1) = c \cdot \frac{\Gamma(a)\,\Gamma(b)}{\Gamma(a+b)},$$

where $\Gamma(x)$ is the gamma function evaluated at the value x. Preliminary trials indicate that by setting a to equal 2 and by varying b and c, a good fit for $A(R)$ could still be achieved. In this case,

$$G(R,2,b,c) = c\int_o^R t(1-t)^{b-1}dt = \frac{c}{(b+1)b}[1-(1+bR)(1-R)^b]$$
$$= c^*[1-(1+bR)(1-R)^b].$$

Now $G(1) = c^*$. Using weighted data from the CPS jurisdictions in the sample, which provided data on reporting, and the BMD07R (BMDX85) nonlinear regression, routine estimates of b and c^* were obtained that minimized the mean square error. A number of different starting values were chosen for b and c^* to demonstrate the stability of the final estimates. The final estimates were:

$b = 138.22$ with standard deviation 28.52
$c^* = .0035293$ with standard deviation .00056

The same relationships exist between c, the rate of confirmation of abuse and neglect reports and d, the identified abuse and neglect rate for any level of reporting. Using the same family of functions as before and the same computational techniques, the final estimates were:

$b = 88.42$ with standard deviation 6.06
$c^* = .02974$ with standard deviation .00196

9. Estimates are based on the number of children under 18 in the United States, as estimated for 1972 (69,016,000). See "Resident Population," *Current Population Reports,* Series P-25, No. 511, Department of Commerce, The U.S. Bureau of the Census (January 1974).

10. Richard J. Light, "Abused and Neglected Children in America: A Study of Alternative Policies," *Harvard Educational Review,* Vol. 43, No. 4 (1973), pp. 556–98.

11. This curve was based upon the relations exhibited by data from this study and a simple projection to estimates of "true" rates of abuse (see Note 8, above).

12. Brian MacMahon et al., *Epidemiological Methods* (Boston: Little, Brown and Company, 1960).

13. *Ibid.*

14. See for example David G. Gil, "Violence Against Children," *Journal of Marriage and the Family,* Vol. 35 (November 1971), pp. 637–48; Alfred Kadushin, *Child Welfare Services,* 2d. ed. (New York: Macmillan Company, 1974).

15. R. J. Gelles, "Child Abuse as Psychopathology—A Sociological Critique and Reformulation," *American Journal of Orthopsychiatry,* Vol. 43, No. 4 (1973), p. 617.

16. Gil, "Violence Against Children," pp. 643–44.

17. Polansky, Hally, and Polansky, *State of Knowledge of Child Neglect,* pp. 30–34.

18. Jeanne M. Giovannoni and A. Billingsley, "Child Neglect Among the Poor: A Study of Parental Inadequacy in Three Ethnic Groups," *Child Welfare,* Vol. 49, No. 4 (1970), pp. 196–204.

19. See, for example, J. J. Spinetta and D. Rigler, "The Child-Abusing Parent: A Psychological Review," *Psychological Bulletin,* Vol. 77, No. 4 (1972), pp. 296–304, and Gelles, "Child Abuse as Psychopathology," p. 617.

20. Abraham Kaplan, *The Conduct of Inquiry: Methodology for Behavioral Science* (San Francisco: Chandler Publishing Company, 1964), p. 298.

21. *Ibid.*

22. See for example Gelles, "Child Abuse as Psychopathology," p. 617, and Spinetta and Rigler, "The Child-Abusing Parent," pp. 296–304.

23. *Ibid.*

24. Gelles, "Child Abuse as Psychopathology," pp. 619–20.

25. The pattern (stress-disorganization-recovery-reorganization) was initially outlined by Earl Loman Koos in *Families in Trouble* (New York: King's Crown Press, 1946) and elaborated by Reuben Hill in "Generic Features of Families Under Stress," *Social Casework,* Vol. 39 (1958), pp. 139–50.

4. PROGRAM STRUCTURE AND PERFORMANCE

1. U.S. Congress, Senate, Committee on Labor and Public Welfare, *Child Abuse Prevention Act: Hearing on PL93–247*, 93d Cong., 1st sess., March 26, 27, 31, and April 24, 1973 (Washington, D.C.: U.S. Government Printing Office), 6:242.

2. See, for example, C. Henry Kempe, "A Practical Approach to the Protection of the Abused Child and Rehabilitation of the Abusing Parent," *Pediatrics,* Vol. 51 (April 1973), pp. 804–12, and Regional Research Institute for Human Services, "Barriers to Planning for Children in Foster Care: A Summary," Portland State University, Portland, Ore., 1976 (mimeographed).

3. U.S., General Accounting Office, *More Can Be Learned and Done About the Well-Being of Children,* Report to the U.S. Congress (Washington, D.C.: U.S. Government Printing Office, 1976).

4. Sanford N. Katz, *When Parents Fail: The Law's Response to Family Breakdown* (Boston: Beacon Press, 1971), p. 9.

5. *Ibid.,* pp. 22–51.

6. *Ibid.,* p. 105.

7. Study, "Freeing Children for Permanent Placement," conducted by the Regional Research Institute for Human Services, Portland State University, Portland, Ore. (mimeographed). Obtained through a visit to the site of the project in 1975.

8. Abraham Kaplan, *The Conduct of Inquiry: Methodology for Behavioral Science* (San Francisco: Chandler Publishing Company, 1964), p. 67.

9. Henry M. Hart, Jr., and John T. McNaughton, "Some Aspects of Evidence and Inference in Law," in *Evidence and Inference,* Daniel Lerner, ed. (Glencoe, Ill.: The Free Press of Glencoe, 1959), pp. 48–72.

10. William J. Gore and J. W. Dyson, eds., *The Making of Decisions* (New York: The Free Press, 1964).

11. Thomas J. Scheff, "Decision Rules: Types of Error and Their Consequences in Medical Diagnosis," in *Mathematical Explorations in Behavioral Science,* Fred Massarik and Philburn Ratoosh, eds. (Homewood, Ill.: Dorsey Press, 1965), p. 69.

12. *Ibid.,* p. 67.

13. Bernard Schwartz, *An Introduction to American Administrative Law* (London: Sir Isaac Pitman and Sons, 1962), pp. 28–29.

14. *Ibid.,* p. 105.

15. Lois G. Forer, "Proposing a Children and Youth Court: A Modest Proposal," in *Legal Rights of Children: Status, Progress and Proposals,* Columbia Human Rights Law Review Staff, eds. (Fair Lawn, N.J., 1972), p. 55.

16. *Ibid.,* p. 53.

17. Katz, *When Parents Fail,* pp. 40–41.

18. Thomas D. Gill, "The Legal Nature of Neglect," quoted in Katz, *When Parents Fail,* p. 65.

19. *Ibid.*

20. C. J. Flammang, *The Police and the Underprotected Child* (Springfield, Ill.: Charles C. Thomas Publishers, 1970), pp. 4–5.

21. Alan Sussman and Stephan J. Cohen, *Reporting Child Abuse and Neglect: Guidelines for Legislation* (Cambridge, Mass.: Ballinger Publishing Company, 1975).

22. Saad Z. Nagi, "Gate-Keeping Decisions in Service Organizations: When Validity Fails," *Human Organization*, Vol. 33, No. 1 (1974), pp. 47–57.

23. Alfred Kadushin, *Child Welfare Services*, 2d ed. (New York: Macmillan Company, 1974).

24. Sol Levine and Paul E. White, "Exchange as a Conceptual Framework for Study of Interorganizational Relationships," *Administrative Science Quarterly*, Vol. 5 (March 1961), pp. 583–601.

25. *Ibid.*

26. William Reid, "Interagency Coordination in Delinquency Prevention and Control," in *Social Welfare Institutions*, Mayer Zald, ed. (New York: John Wiley and Sons, 1965), p. 357.

27. *Ibid.*

28. *Ibid.*

29. Violet M. Seider, "Some Essentials in Planning Rehabilitation Services," *Rehabilitation Literature*, Vol. 25, No. 3 (1964), pp. 66–70.

30. Eugene Litwak and Lydia R. Hylton, "Interorganizational Analysis: A Hypothesis on Coordinating Agencies," *Administrative Science Quarterly*, Vol. 6 (March 1962), pp. 395–420.

31. William Reid, "Interagency Coordination," pp. 365–66.

5. TOWARD ENHANCED COPING

1. U.S. Congress, Senate, Committee on Labor and Public Welfare, *Child Abuse Prevention Act: Hearing on PL93–247*, 93d Cong., 1st sess., March 26, 27, 31, and April 24, 1973 (Washington, D.C.: U.S. Government Printing Office), p. 246.

2. See, for example, Lenore C. Terr and A. S. Watson, "The Battered Child Rebrutalized: 10 Cases of Medical-Legal Confusion," *American Journal of Psychiatry*, Vol. 124, No. 10 (1968); and Clara L. Johnson, *Two Community Protective Service Systems: Comparative Evaluation of Systems Operations* (Athens, Ga.: Regional Institute of Social Welfare Research, University of Georgia, 1976).

3. See Alan Sussman and Stephan J. Cohen, *Reporting Child Abuse and Neglect: Guidelines for Legislation* (Cambridge, Mass.: Ballinger Publishing Company, 1975).

4. *Ibid.*, p. 12.

5. Marvin R. Burt and Louis H. Blair, *Options for Improving the Care of Neglected and Dependent Children* (Washington, D.C.: The Urban Institute, 1971).

6. Harold Lasswell, as quoted by James Arthur Robinson in *Congress and Foreign Policy Making* (Homewood, Ill.: Dorsey Press, 1962), p. 6.

7. See, for example, Francis G. Caro, ed., *Readings in Evaluation Research* (New York: Russell Sage Foundation, 1971); Peter H. Rossi and Walter Williams, eds., *Evaluating Social Programs: Theory, Practice, and Politics* (New York: Seminar Press, 1972); Edward A. Suchman, *Evaluative Research: Principles and Practice in Public Service and Social Action Programs* (New York: Russell Sage Foundation, 1967); Carol H. Weiss, *Evaluation Research: Methods of Assessing Program Effectiveness* (Englewood Cliffs, N.J.: Prentice-Hall, 1972); and Walter Williams, *Social Policy Research and Analysis* (New York: American Elsevier Publishing Company, 1971).

INDEX